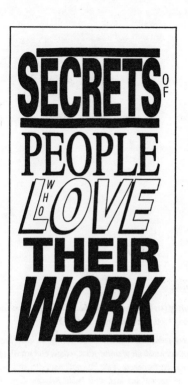

SECRETS OF PEOPLE WHO LOVE THEIR WORK

Janis Long Harris

INTERVARSITY PRESS
DOWNERS GROVE, ILLINOIS 60515

InterVarsity Press is the book-publishing division of InterVarsity Christian Fellowship, a student movement active on campus at hundreds of universities, colleges and schools of nursing in the United States of America, and a member movement of the International Fellowship of Evangelical Students. For information about local and regional activities, write Public Relations Dept., InterVarsity Christian Fellowship, 6400 Schroeder Rd., P.O. Box 7895, Madison, WI 53707-7895.

All Scripture quotations, unless otherwise indicated, are from the HOLY BIBLE, NEW INTERNATIONAL VERSION. Copyright © 1973, 1978, 1984 International Bible Society. Used by permission of Zondervan Publishing House. All rights reserved.

Cover illustration: Ed Killeen

ISBN 0-8308-1388-8

Printed in the United States of America ∞

Library of Congress Cataloging-in-Publication Data

Harris, Janis Long, 1951-
    Secrets of people who love their work/by Janis Long Harris.
        p.   cm.
    ISBN 0-8308-1388-8
    1. Vocational interests—Case studies.   2. Vocation—Case studies.
    3. Job satisfaction—Case studies.   I. Title.
    HF5381.5.H365   1992
    331.7'02—dc20   *92-8605*
                                                                    CIP

17	16	15	14	13	12	11	10	9	8	7	6	5	4	3	2	1
05	04	03	02	01	00	99	98	97	96	95	94	93	92			

To Paul, who supported my quest
to find work I could love,
and Janet,
who is still on the journey

Introduction

*The hatred of work must be one of
the most depressing consequences of the Fall.*
**DOROTHY L. SAYERS,
THE ZEAL OF THY HOUSE**

I'VE NEVER BEEN ABLE TO RECONCILE MYSELF TO THE IDEA THAT WORK is, by its very nature, unpleasant.

I know, I know: ever since the Fall, we humans have had to labor by the sweat of our brows, as Genesis put it. "Laboring by the sweat of the brow" means there will always be an odious quality to work, or so I'm told.

And yet, I am obsessed with work. A child of my culture, I've spent more than half my years on earth preparing to do it, and now I expect it to bring me not only a decent income, but enjoyment, fulfillment and an identity.

I'm not alone. It strikes me how many people I know who are on a continuing quest for meaningful, satisfying work—how many people who would give almost anything to be able to say, "I love my work."

Those of us who are Christians have an added element of pressure in our quest, a sense of urgency about finding work that is not just a career, but a spiritual calling, a true vocation. Just finding work we can like is hard enough.

Often, the assumption is that there is a particular kind of job or workplace that will be conducive to satisfying work. And much has been written about conditions in the workplace that contribute to employee satisfaction. But little has been written about the characteristics of people who enjoy their work.

Then too, every bookstand has at least one volume, usually more, about the characteristics of people who achieve career success. The implicit assumption is that achievement brings with it happiness and satisfaction. Yet most of us know many people who are "successful" in the sense that they have achieved position, money, status and power, but who take little pleasure in their work. I also know people who have few of the traditional trappings of success who would say without hesitation that they love their work.

What are the secrets of people, especially people of faith, who love their work—who know they've found their calling? Do they share any common characteristics? Is there anything to be learned from them that would enable others to love their work or find work they can love?

Fascinated by these questions, I began interviewing people, primarily—though not exclusively—people with a strong Christian faith who say they love their work. I wanted to know how they found their vocation, how they view their work in the context of their lives, how their faith fits into the picture.

It was exhilarating to find, as I talked with these work lovers, that several recurring themes emerged in their conversation. I heard certain words and phrases and story lines over and over again. I became convinced that there are some commonalities among people who love their work—and that discovering these commonalities could be of help to others who *want* to love their work.

Although the people interviewed for this book share many common characteristics, they are also very diverse. The interview group included people in the professions, people who work with their hands, business executives, teachers, artists and full-time Christian workers. I talked to people who make a lot of money and people who make very little money. People with power and prestige and people without it. Men and women. Older people and younger people.

The interview process was hardly scientific. I simply asked these people to tell me their stories and offer any advice they might want to share. The people I talked to were, for the most part, people I know, or friends of people I know. Consequently, their experiences—and my conclusions—are undoubtedly most characteristic of middle-class Americans. The themes that popped up consistently throughout the interviews became the chapter topics in this book.

While I was working on this project, I talked with some people who questioned the premise that work can or should be consistently enjoyable. Searching for fulfillment in work, they said, is like searching for happiness—the more you pursue it, the more it eludes you.

Perhaps. It may be that people who love their work are the exceptions, that the folks I interviewed have achieved a level of vocational satisfaction most of us are unlikely to attain. But after talking with scores of work lovers, I'm convinced that we can learn from them—that in following their example, we can derive *more* satisfaction from work.

In fact, writing this book changed *my* work life rather dramatically. Interviewing people who genuinely loved their work made me realize the extent to which I did not love my own. When I started this book, I had a good position as a fund raiser with a large social service organization. I was enjoying success, had just been promoted and, on the basis of all outward appearances, should have been very happy. But I was inexplicably dissatisfied—at least in my work life. As I observed more and more work lovers, however, and listened to their stories, I began to sense that God was talking to me through them, that he was showing me some of the reasons for my dissatisfaction with work. Cynic that I am, I also considered the possibility that the notion God was speaking to me was all just wishful thinking on my part. But whether it was the voice of God, or just common sense, I increasingly came to believe I should follow the example of the people who were telling me their stories, people who loved their work a whole lot more than I loved mine.

In other words, I needed to be more open to hearing the voice of God. Draw on my "gifted passions." Pay attention to models, mentors and voices of affirmation. Take risks. Find community. Develop my level of competence. Take more seriously the importance of the money variable. Express my faith through my work. Make sacrifices. Believe my work was important. Find balance between work and other important aspects of life. Find not only the right process, but the right place to exercise that process.

After a lot of soul searching and praying and foot dragging and second guessing, I realized that doing these things meant leaving my job and going out on my own as a writer. So I did. At the time, it felt like I was jumping off a cliff. But the past year, though not without difficulties, has brought as much or more work satisfaction than I've ever experienced previously. And I feel a sense of profound gratitude to God and to the people who shared their stories with me. Perhaps you are in the same place I was when I started researching this book—dissatisfied with work, but not sure why or what to do about it. Or maybe you're a young person who is still in the process of making decisions about your life's work. I can't guarantee that reading this book will affect your life as significantly as writing it affected me. After all, it contains very few "how to" formulas. Rather, it offers stories and pieces of advice from people of faith who have been willing to share the secrets of their journeys toward meaningful, satisfying, "lovable" work.

But stories have power. My hope is that the stories of these work lovers will inform *your* journey, as they have mine.

1

Voices
& the Leading
of God

---

*As a Christian, I believe that God has a purpose
for my life. But he doesn't say, "Go be a math professor."
You have to follow a sense of appropriateness,
oughtness, correctness.*

COLLEGE PROFESSOR

---

*I heard a voice from God. It wasn't audible,
but like someone whispering in my ear.*

DIALYSIS NURSE

---

*The world is full of people who seem to have listened
to the wrong voice and are now engaged in life-work in which
they find no pleasure or purpose.*

**FREDERICK BUECHNER,
THE HUNGERING DARK**

THIS IS NOT A BOOK ABOUT DISCOVERING GOD'S WILL FOR YOUR LIFE,
at least not primarily. But people of faith who love their work are,
for the most part, people who can point to God's guidance in
finding their vocation. They are people who have heard God
speak, sometimes directly, sometimes indirectly. They are people
who have been able to recognize God's voice—in their own inner
voice, in words of encouragement from a trusted friend or advisor,

in circumstances. Perhaps even more important, they are people who have been able to resist the voices of a culture that tells them they must find a vocation that will bring them power and money and status, rather than a vocation that fits their gifts, brings them joy and feels worth doing.

The Inner Voice

Richard Blackburn is a high-school English and humanities teacher in his mid-thirties. Passionate about his work, Rich's athletic good looks and dramatic teaching style make him a Pied Piper in the classroom. He loves literature. He loves his students. He loves teaching. But he almost missed his calling.

"I made the mistake of not listening to some inner passions early enough," says Rich. "Although I was impressed with some of my teachers early on, for some reason I never looked at education. It was going to be engineering, business or pre-med. Financial motivation was one factor—I knew exactly what I would do with extra money, everything from Jaguars to touring castles in my spare time. So in college, I started taking some of the driest economics courses in the world—and spent the rest of my time lying under a tree reading Tolkien and C. S. Lewis. I should have realized some things a little bit earlier."

Following college, Rich spent several frustrating years as a salesman in the family business before deciding, at age twenty-six, to make a career switch to teaching. "I finally decided to listen to the inner voice—what Joseph Campbell might call one's center and what we with a spiritual orientation might call the guidance of the Spirit," he explains.

But after teaching for two years, Rich began to question his calling and started looking for a sales position again. "I went with a company at a time when they were just opening up their operations on university campuses," he recalls. "Notice what's happening in my mind here—I'm staying close to education, and I'm still going to rake in some big bucks. I had been on the job for about six months when we were sent as part of a sales and engineering team to a college in Wisconsin. One beautiful sunlit afternoon, I had about ten minutes waiting for another appointment so, as we walked by an open classroom, I walked in. I remember it had old English paneling and a lectern in front of all these desks. It was a magic moment. James Joyce would call it one of his epiphanies. Suddenly, the whole universe was screaming at me—'What are you doing? Get yourself back to that lectern! Get yourself walking in those aisles!'

"Usually those thunderbolt moments don't happen. But if there was a thunderbolt moment in my life, that was it. If there was anything my fixation on big bucks needed, it was that."

Blackburn is right. Thunderbolt moments don't happen very often—few of the people interviewed for this book experienced them. If their experience is any guide, God is reluctant to shout to get his point across. But he sometimes whispers—and people of faith who love their work are people who can hear those whispers.

"Sometimes I tell people, 'Yes, I heard a voice from God,' " jokes Telva Urban, a dialysis nurse at a large academic medical center, who says her love for her work is a pleasant surprise. "But that's kind of the feeling I got. People think I'm nuts. It wasn't audible, but like someone whispering in my ear, 'Try being a nurse.' I had the same sensation when I saw the ad for a dialysis nurse. I don't tell that to many people, but I did have that kind of a feeling."

Frequently, people who love their work listened to an inner voice, a voice they came to recognize as the voice of God, which spoke to them over a period of time. That was the case for Gary Ginter, one of the founding partners of CRT, an extremely successful commodities firm which has been portrayed by the national media as something of a Wall Street miracle story. Gary was attending Bible school with the intention of becoming a missionary when he became convinced that God was calling him to go into business.

"I had a clarity, a certainty that developed over a period of a year," he recalls. "I experienced firsthand the verse in Philippians that says, 'God is at work within you both to will and do his own good pleasure.' He had to do that because I had no interest in business. But he called me into it, working it out that I also enjoyed it. He gave me a pleasure that continues to this day, because I love business with a passion." David Hogue, an intense man in his forties who directs the counseling center at a large Midwestern church, has come to rely on his inner voice, seeing it as one of the ways in which God speaks to him. "I think there is a sense, some kind of driving thing inside me, that almost decides intuitively what to do next," he says. "I didn't even go through career evaluation, which is something I do for other people. There is just kind of an internal sense."

Other Voices

As people of faith who love their work talk about finding their calling, one of the most frequent themes that emerges is that of "other voices"—voices of people who affirmed their strengths or pointed the way to a path they wouldn't have seen on their own.

For Rich Blackburn, it was the voice of a friend who first affirmed his gifts and put him in touch with his own inner voice. "A psychologist friend of the family came to me and said, 'You know, you have a real gift of teaching; have you ever considered a teaching career?' That was one of the first point-blank challenges I'd ever had," says Rich, "and it struck me strong enough to dilute my financial motivations." Outside voices were also influential in guiding pastoral counselor David Hogue. David has so many gifts and interests that, as a young person, it was difficult choosing a college major, much less a career path. He excelled in, among other areas, math, physics, English and music. A high-school counselor told him, "This is going to be tough for you because there are any number of things you could do. It's harder counseling someone like you than somebody who has only one or two areas they are really very good in."

David struggled to find direction but, after going through several different majors, began to develop a sense of call in his sophomore year in college.

"Following a mission trip to Haiti," he says, "I became convinced that my call was to the mission field. That lasted about five months for me and then became more of a general sense of call to ministry—a call that was confirmed by one of the members of the faculty, a professor who told somebody else, 'Let's pray that David ends up in the ministry.' When I heard this story, it was very influential. Here was a man I admired tremendously, and it seemed to me that he had seen something that I hadn't seen."

Circumstances and the Voice of God

People of faith who love their work are open to hearing the voice of God in the circumstances of their lives. They actively look for meaning in events. David Hogue: "I think I have really paid attention to circumstances which presented themselves as possibly the voice of God. I've tried to understand the message in events, things offered or withheld. When circumstances line up with my inside experience, I feel I'm on the right track."

For some work lovers, circumstances confirmed an existing sense of calling or guidance. Rich Blackburn, for example, found that success came easily and quickly when he followed his call into teaching. "All the cards immediately fell my way when I listened to the inner voice," he says. For him, success was a confirmation of his calling.

But for others, the circumstances through which they heard the voice of God were very different. God speaks through failure as well as success, as David Orth, an award-winning woodworker, can testify. David tells his own story:

"I didn't see woodworking as a way to make a living. It was just something I loved. So I buckled down to study philosophy, which was very interesting to me, but it was so intellectual, so rarefied. And here I was, really at heart someone who was at home and in love with craft, manipulating wood, the feel of wood, the smell of it—here I was, sitting in an armchair, hardly able to get through the academic side of the thing I was pursuing.

"Anyway, I didn't consider woodworking because it seemed so blue collar. My dad had a doctorate. Everyone around me was going to graduate school and getting higher degrees. So I went on to graduate school in philosophy. It was a very painful experience, though I loved it at a certain level. What I loved was finding answers to my own questions. I had my own personal questions, and that's what I was geared toward.

"When it came to the preliminary examinations for getting into the doctorate program, I looked at these questions and I hadn't studied for them. They were abstract, totally uninteresting and boring.

"I failed the exams the first time around. I tried hard the second year, studied hard to be able to perform like a philosopher should, to be able to answer anybody's abstract questions. But it just wasn't in me. I wasn't interested in Plato and Aristotle. I was interested in Heidegger and Michael Polanyi, modern philosophers beginning to talk about craft and art as an important thing. I was excited about this, but none of those questions showed up on the test. I think I could have been a good philosopher if there had been a way within the system to follow where my joy was, but there wasn't.

"So philosophy finally gave me a road out of philosophy. I began to find philosophers who talked about beauty and craft and the philosophy of technology as a whole era of philosophy that was opening up. I ate this stuff up. At the same time, I began to pick up my interest in craft. When I inherited my grandfather's tools, I set up a shop in my garage. I'd come home from graduate school and spend four hours in the shop, building beautiful tables. To me it was all the same thing. Here I was reading Heidegger about the artist and craftsman and equipment or Michael Polanyi on tacit knowledge—more right-brain knowledge that you can't verbalize, but you can say, for example, with your hands. I felt that in some ways I was doing philosophy when I came home.

"I didn't pass my preliminary exams for the second time. It was terribly shameful. I think a lot of forces in society make you ashamed of the thing that gives you bliss and force you to take on another persona. I had taken on another persona, that of this abstract kind of person, and it just wasn't me. But I have gratitude for those years because it certainly influenced my work. Evil never has the last say. Things do work together for good. I think I would have stuck it out in philosophy because of my ego if I hadn't failed these tests. I see that failing as a severe mercy, something that had to happen to get me back on track."

Dr. Melicent Huneycutt, formerly a missionary and college English professor, and currently pastor of spiritual life at a large Midwestern church, is a tall, dignified woman with a soft southern accent who quietly exudes her love for her work. Now in her early sixties, she has followed the voice of God in and out of several vocations, hearing him speak in a variety of ways.

"I've experienced God's guidance mostly through circumstances and frequently through somebody else's insight," she observes. "For example, I was working as a director of Christian growth when my senior pastor came to see me one day and said, 'Have you ever considered ordination?' I was startled because it was a new idea for women to be ordained in our denomination. I said, 'No, I'm so happy doing what I am, and I feel respected and honored in the place that I'm in. I don't think I need any more authority or authentication. I'm content.'

"But within two months after he said that to me, several things happened. One was a call from a young woman who I had counseled with for many years because she had been abused as a child. As my student in college, she had been so afraid of men that she'd been unable to take a test in the same room as a boy. So we always had to give her exams in a separate room. She called to say she was getting married and was happy and she wanted me to do the ceremony. I had to say no because I couldn't do ceremonies.

"A lady whom I loved very much, an older woman who had outlived all of her family, was dying and talked to me about whether or not to have the support systems removed and just put her life in the hands of God. She decided to do that and asked me to stay with her as long as she was alive. Which I did. She asked me to do her funeral. I couldn't. And I thought, *God is saying something to me. I've started something I can't complete.* I wanted to stay with these people all the way through the movement of their lives that God has made me part of. So I began to seek ordination at that time.

"Sometimes my guidance had been just a sense of call, for example, when I saw that my ability to teach teachers to teach really opened the door to my mission work in Korea after the war. It was as if I had to do this. I'm equipped to, I want to. I have a desire and excitement about it. Everything in me is just pulled and tugged. It would have been very hard for me not to have done it. So sometimes there was a sense of pretty direct call—seeing that a need and my gifts matched. But that is sometimes like a will o' the wisp that leads you astray, because I find that sometimes when I start putting together a need and my abilities, I come up with a false sense of call and burn out. That happens when I'm trying to do more than I'm really called to do.

"I find that I have to test every new wave of my ministry or calling. Usually through common sense. I talk to other people. Again, I think a lot of my sense of vocation comes out of a sense of community. Just at every step it's been the shaping influence of a community of faith—the people around me—their needs, their insights or their wisdom. My mother and dad. A missionary who came to stay with us when I was a child who really got me excited about missions. So that one of the things I try to do is keep a group of people around me whom I can trust for advice and guidance when I'm not sure what the next step ought to be."

People of faith who love their work are people who are open to hearing the voice of God. Often, they've been able to hear him speak—sometimes in shouts and sometimes in whispers—in their own inner voice. Some experience the inner voice as a natural preference. Others hear it as an almost audible suggestion, a persistent thought that pops into their head. Still others perceive it as a compelling sense of directedness—or just an intuitive feeling.

People of faith who love their work may hear God speak in the voice of others—teachers, parents, friends, counselors—people who know them well and are able to point out gifts and interests they may not be able to recognize in themselves.

People of faith who love their work hear the voice of God in circumstances. Sometimes those circumstances take the form of success experiences which confirm a sense of direction. Sometimes they are circumstances of failure, severe mercies which painfully but effectively serve to bring the prospective work lover back on track.

God speaks to us all in different ways—occasionally through thunderbolt moments or whispers in the ear, more frequently through quiet epiphanies, often through success and failure. If we listen, we can hear him, and sometimes he's telling us secrets about how to find the kind of work we were created to do—work we can love.

2

Models, Mentors & Voices of Affirmation

CALVIN LONG WAS FLOUNDERING. HE WAS WELL INTO COLLEGE, BUT HE couldn't decide on a major. Music was one option. After all, he loved singing in the choir. The music they sang was so beautiful it made the hair on the back of his neck stand on end. But as he looked around at his fellow choir members, he realized that most of them had, as he puts it, "more talent in their little fingers" than he had in his whole body. He could read music and sing pretty well, but they could take an instrument and improvise and be creative in a way he never could. Discouraged, he spilled out his dilemma to one of his favorite teachers, a math professor. "Cal," the professor responded, "you're very gifted in math. Why don't you become a mathematician?" "But what would I do to make a living?" Cal replied. "What do you think I do?" his professor retorted. Cal thought about that. He liked math. He did well in it. Why not become a mathematician?

The story of how Calvin Long decided to pursue a career in math reminds me of an observation my brother made years ago: People tend to aspire to familiar roles. If you don't know any lawyers, for example, you're less likely to make a career in law your goal than someone whose father or uncle or family friend is an attorney. Unless, of course, someone you respect points out what a good lawyer you would make—and helps you with some of the practical steps to becoming a lawyer. It's not surprising, then, that models, mentors and voices of affirmers play such an important role in the stories of so many people who love their work.

Woodworker David Orth is a good example. "I think a lot of people who want to get into woodworking struggle because they weren't brought up with it," he says. "Building something is a mystery to them, a frightening thing. To me it was something close. My grandfather, for example, was an amateur woodworker. He had a garage full of tools, and he loved to spend lots of time back there. I didn't get to help all that much but I spent a lot of time watching. I think that's real important. Even though you may not have the skills to do something yet, you've seen it happen.

"When we moved to Central America where my folks were missionaries, woodworking was very much a part of the society. It seemed like there were little woodshops on every corner. It was cheaper to have someone build you a table than to go and buy it in the store. Crafts were just accepted as a routine part of life. So I have a lot of gratitude for having been able to grow up in that kind of culture.

"I also grew up with a mother who is an artist. She does watercolors mostly and interior design. She's just in love with beauty and beautiful things, even though they never cost much. So when I would draw a picture or something as a kid, I would get praised.

"Then, after I grew up and had my own woodworking shop, there was this woodworker I would see in the *Chicago Tribune* every once in a while. I saw him one day in a gallery that was showing woodworking and went up and introduced myself very shyly. Even though I had my own shop, I didn't consider myself in any way an artist at that point—I was just building furniture. But I happened to have some snapshots of my work, and I pulled them out and he looked at them and said, 'You should have been showing your work here. You should have been in the show.' I walked out on three feet of air because of the remark this guy had made. Here was someone I looked up to who validated my work.

"Looking back," David observes, "I can see that I was given a lot of gifts through these people and situations. And I feel tremendous gratitude for that."

Greg Darnieder's story is also one of models, mentors and affirmers. Growing up in a Catholic family in Oshkosh, Wisconsin, Greg's first model was his uncle, a priest with a social conscience. When his uncle got involved with helping migrant workers who picked cucumbers in Wisconsin, Greg would go along with him to visit the migrant camps. "It was my first view of a world that wasn't this ideal, no-concerns life that's just there to be enjoyed," recalls Greg. Later, in college, Greg met his second role model, Tom O'Brian, a Christian Brother who ran a summer program for inner-city kids in a "slum ghetto" of St. Louis. Greg and about twenty other college students worked in the program, tutoring the kids in the morning and taking them to a camp outside the city in the afternoon. "We literally lived in slum housing down there," recalls Greg, "but the whole experience just totally enraptured me. I had a real sense that this was the beginning of something. Going down there gave me a sense of purpose. And Tom had such an effect on my life that I thought, *Well, the way to live my life would be as a Christian Brother. To basically give my life away.* Because he did."

Greg changed his mind about a professional religious vocation a year later, but he persisted in his determination to sacrifice his life in the service of others. After graduating from college, he taught school in a poor neighborhood of St. Louis. Then he got married and went to graduate school. While studying for a master's in Christian education at Wheaton College, he met an urban pastor named Bill Leslie—his third model and mentor. "Bill was teaching this class in urban life," explains Greg. "It wasn't even a class I was supposed to take, but the class I *was* supposed to take had already filled up. Anyway, because of that exposure, my wife and I started to attend the church Bill pastored in downtown Chicago."

It happened that the church was looking for someone to direct its tutoring program for poor inner-city kids. Greg applied and got the job, accepting Bill's challenge of making a minimum commitment of five years to the position. That was fourteen years ago. Since then, with frequent doses of affirmation from Bill Leslie, Greg has nurtured what used to be a tiny tutoring program with a budget of $24,000 a year into a highly respected, multi-faceted educational ministry with 175 employees and a budget of over a million dollars. And he loves his work. It never would have happened, says Greg, if it hadn't been for the modeling and mentoring and affirmation he received from his uncle and Tom O'Brian and Bill Leslie.

Sandy Rios says she never intended to be a professional singer, but so many people encouraged and pushed and dragged her into using her gifts that she almost had no choice. It started back in college, when Sandy met her first mentor, Dr. Warren Angell. "He was a silver-haired dynamo who directed the Men's Glee Club. Even though it was a men's choir, they had seven girl singers they called The Little Sisters. I auditioned and made it in and Dean Angell was just incredible to me. He used to tell me when I got on stage, 'Sandy, you just light up!' No one else had ever believed in me like that. He would push me to do things I wouldn't have ever done otherwise. I was embarrassed and I'd say, 'Let somebody else sing. Let so-and-so have the solo.' But he would just insist. He was definitely my cheerleader, my encourager."

More encouragers came into Sandy's life after she married and had children. John Wilson, editor of a music publishing company, director of a respected Christian singing group and, like Sandy, parent of a disabled child, gave her a chance to sing with his group, which led to recording opportunities and a job as his replacement directing a college choir. Jim Warren, host of "Prime Time America," a radio program heard on Christian stations across the country, invited her to fill in as co-host of the program after hearing her sing and speak at a Sunday-evening church service. Then he invited her back again and again—and Sandy discovered that her true gift isn't just music, but communication.

Sandy, Greg and David are work lovers today in part because of the role that other people—models, mentors and affirmers—played in their lives. But what are models, mentors and affirmers exactly?

Models
Models are those people whose very lives create new possibilities for us. They are the people who show us how to dream. They are people like Dean Leuking's uncle.

"I went to high school during World War 2, and I wasn't too sure what I wanted to do with my life," says Dean, now a veteran pastor. "I was a year too young to be drafted, so I didn't go into the service. I had an interest in law, and having worked during the summers for an uncle who was a farmer I was also thinking about agriculture. But I had another uncle who was a pastor in Illinois. He was also a former professional baseball player and, since I had an opportunity to sign a contract with the Philadelphia Phillies when I was in my late teens, I was always interested in anybody who had been in baseball. So I listened when he very quietly told me from time to time how much pastoral ministry meant to him. He never once said, 'Why don't you do this?' He just said what it meant to him."

Dean's baseball-playing, ministry-loving uncle was a winsome role model who, like other role models, served as a picture through which God could speak. Work lovers are people who have had eyes to see God's message in the picture.

Affirmers

Affirmers are people whose voices give shape to our dreams. By identifying or confirming our gifts, affirmers help us hear God's call in our lives.

The entire direction of Peter Baker's medical career was changed as a result of an affirmer. As an intern, Peter had already decided he wanted to specialize in internal medicine—"the queen of medicine." But while he was doing the pediatrics portion of his internship, the head of the department took him aside and said, "You look like you have fun with those kids. Have you thought about being a pediatrician?"

"I really hadn't," recalls Peter, "but his personal interest and encouragement had a lot to do with my changing my mind very quickly. I went up and cancelled my plans to study internal medicine and signed up for the pediatrics program instead."

A model-turned-affirmer was instrumental in Rich Blackburn's decision to leave the family business and go into teaching. "I was very impressed with a family friend who was not only a psychologist but also an amazing teacher and great discussion facilitator," says Rich. "Here I was selling products—lumber and cubic yards of cement—while he was helping people turn their lives around, helping them be effective as human beings. He was aware of some teaching I was doing at a local church and also some coaching activities, and one day he came to me and said, 'You know, you have a real gift of teaching. Have you ever considered a career in this?' That pointblank challenge struck me hard enough to dilute some of my financial motivations for staying in business. I eventually decided to listen to the inner voice and at age twenty-six, I made a career switch."

David Horner, president of North Park College, says he has a deep sense of indebtedness to the many people who took an interest in him as a young man and helped him along his vocational journey. He points to two affirmers in particular whose voices guided him in the direction of educational administration. "I was a fairly recent graduate of Barrington College when they tapped me to be the volunteer director of their annual fund-raising campaign," recalls David. "I gave a little speech at one of the banquets and the former president of the college came up to me afterwards and said, 'You have a real gift of persuading people and you ought to develop it.'

"Another conversation I had that was really helpful to me," continues David, "was one I had with the former president of Providence College. He was a distinguished visiting professor at the University of Rhode Island when I was a grad student there. We actually shared an office because I was a teaching assistant. I talked with him about my interest in the academic world and yet my uncertainty about being a pure academic, about how I enjoyed business. He really encouraged me to think about a career in academic administration because it would place me in a context I seemed to enjoy but with tasks that were more common to the business experience. He said, 'Higher education is going to face a lot of challenges, and what it is really going to need are people who have a real feel for the academic world, but who also have sophisticated training as administrators and managers. I know you well enough to know that you've got academe in your heart—you know what makes it tick intuitively. If you take that intuition and blend it with sophisticated administrative training, I think you could really have something special to offer.' Explicit comments like that have been very helpful in guiding me."

Affirmers are voices through whom God speaks. Work lovers are people who have been able to hear God in the voices.

Mentors

Mentors show us how to achieve our dreams. They are not only models and affirmers, but teachers and cheerleaders. They critique. They pat on the back. They show us how to do it. And they give us opportunities to do it.

Chuck Swirsky might never have fulfilled his dream of becoming a sports broadcaster if it hadn't been for a series of mentors, the first of whom came into his life the summer he was twelve years old. Chuck was staying with his uncle's family in Baltimore for a month. The uncle was a teacher, and it turned out that the father of one of his students was Vince Bagli, a TV sportscaster. One thing led to another and Chuck ended up spending the month following Vince around as he worked.

"I went everywhere with him," recalls Chuck. "I went to the TV station with him and saw how he prepared his copy. I went out to the ballpark and saw him do interviews. Here I am twelve years old going from Memorial Stadium in Baltimore where he interviewed Brooks Robinson, to the Colts training camp where he talked to Johnny Unitas, to the Bullets summer camp where he interviewed a lot of other great stars. Because of that relationship, I came back really knowing that was exactly what I wanted to do."

Vince Bagli invited Chuck back to visit every summer and introduced him to a second important mentor, Ernie Harwell, a member of the Baseball Hall of Fame and voice of the Tigers.

"I would sit in the broadcast booth when the Tigers were in town and Ernie would put me right next to him," says Chuck. "I would have to use a phone book in order to see the ballpark, but Ernie was right there. This man was unbelievable. He wrote me every month. He stayed in touch with me and saw my progression through elementary school, junior high, high school, college and the beginning of my career in Seattle. We'd get together when the Tigers played the Mariners. When I was in college in Ohio, I'd drive up to Cleveland to see him. And later in Chicago, when the Tigers came to play the Sox. Ernie has known me for over twenty years, and he's had a profound effect."

Ron Nikkel, president of Prison Fellowship International, talks about the role that mentors have played in his life: "There have been a number of people who have been tremendous mentors and encouragers to me," he says. "They've each helped me in different ways—sometimes by giving me opportunities to take leadership, sometimes encouraging me to try something new. I think the thing that has been most affirming and fairly consistent in a lot of my experience is that I've worked with people who gave me the opportunity to fail. They weren't controlling managers. They didn't stifle the call of God in my life.

"I think that Jay Kesler, for example, was a real mentor when I worked for Youth for Christ. Jay drew out my creativity. He encouraged innovation. He modeled how to think about things from a nontraditional Christian perspective."

Ken Phillips is another work lover who testifies to the influence that mentors can have in shaping a vocation. He remembers a family friend, a psychologist, who took an interest in him while he was in medical school—allowing him to work with him as a cotherapist in group therapy situations one summer. "It had very little to do with medical school," says Ken, "but I found that I really enjoyed it. That, plus the fact that he believed in me and believed I could do this if I wanted to, was very instrumental in my decision to become a psychiatrist."

Mentors are like parents through whom God nurtures our gifts.

Mentors don't give us our gifts, but they help us recognize and develop and use the ones we've been given. Work lovers are people who have the heart to respond to God by responding to the nurturing people he has put in their path.

You may not have an abundance of models, affirmers and mentors in your life. But if you pay attention, you can probably find someone to serve in at least one of these roles.

Is there someone in your life for whom you have unusual respect, someone whose life and vocation is particularly attractive to you? Consider the possibility of looking to that person as a role model.

Have you ever received a particularly meaningful compliment about your talents or abilities from someone you admire and whose judgment you trust? Perhaps you've been blessed with an affirmer, someone whose encouragement can serve to focus and fuel your vocational direction.

Is there anyone you know who can show you how to achieve your dreams, who's accomplished what you want to accomplish and can tell you or show you how to move along your vocational path? Perhaps that person is a potential mentor. Don't be afraid to ask such a person for advice or help—he or she is more likely to be flattered than annoyed.

Models, mentors, affirmers—they are the pictures, the voices and the nurturers God uses to guide us to vocation. Do you have the eyes to see, the ears to hear, and the heart to respond?

3

Discovering
Your Gifted
Passions

——————

MODELS, MENTORS AND AFFIRMERS ARE SOME OF THE OUTSIDE VOICES
God uses to direct us as we seek to find—and use—our gifts. But
it's only when he speaks to us through the inner voice that we learn
to recognize our gifted passions. And discovering and using gifted
passions is one of the most important secrets of people who love
their work.

At age thirty-eight, Dick Winzeler is blond, fit, handsome. He
looks as if he should portray a high-school football coach on a
prime time television series. Perhaps someday he will, because Dick
is forging a living as a Hollywood actor, writer and musician.

Dick, who almost became a high-school physical education
teacher in real life, is in love with the creative process. He is passionate about writing, acting and creating music. What's more, he
is gifted in all three areas. Dick, like most people who love their
work, possesses gifted passions.

What Is a Gifted Passion?

When your gifts and your passions converge, you have a gifted passion—a passion supported by your gifts. If you desperately love to paint and are talented as a painter, you have a gifted passion. If you derive great pleasure from teaching and have a knack for communicating with students, you have a gifted passion. If you can't imagine anything more fun than telling a computer what to do and you possess the logic and mental stamina necessary for computer programming, you have a gifted passion. If you have a gifted passion and are able to incorporate it into your vocation you have a very good chance of loving your work. But if your vocation is based on gifts alone, without passion, or passions that are not supported by gifts, it's unlikely that you'll be able to love your work—at least not for very long.

Woodworker David Orth is passionate about music and once thought that he wanted to be a composer—until he discovered that his love for music wasn't adequately supported by his gifts. "I wanted dearly to write music," he recalls, "but I just didn't have it in me. Music was a deeply moving thing to me. I could play it with great feeling. But I couldn't write it to save my life. Imagine my surprise when I woke up one day and realized that in woodworking I was no longer just copying, but coming up with original ideas and making things that were beautiful, things that had come out of my own heart. I finally realized that what I was trying to do with music I could do with woodworking." David had to give up the dream of pursuing one of his passions, at least vocationally, because it wasn't his *gifted* passion. But in woodworking he found an activity where his gifts and his passion converged. He now derives deep satisfaction from his vocation as a professional woodworker, satisfaction he never could have obtained if he had continued his struggle to write music.

Some people possess the gifts to do a particular kind of work, but have no heart for it—and consequently are unable to love it as a vocation. Take, for example, Dr. Peter Baker, who was an engineer before he decided to go to medical school. He was a competent engineer, but he didn't enjoy engineering. Today, he's an equally competent pediatrician who loves going to work every day. The same intellectual and problem-solving abilities that made him a good engineer make him a good doctor. He has the gifts to pursue either profession. But he has a passion for pediatrics. He loves kids. He's fascinated by their emotional and physical development. He takes great pleasure in his day-to-day contacts with his young patients and their parents. He loves his work—because he was able to distinguish between his gifts and his gifted passions.

Dick Winzeler almost missed finding his vocation as a creative artist and performer because he confused his gifts with his gifted passions. Dick is one of those rare people who seem to be talented at everything they try. High-school classmates remember him as a kind of teen-age Renaissance man. Sports, music, academics, writing, drama—Dick could do it all, and do it well. But when he could do so many things so well, it was hard to sort out what he really *wanted* to do. It was hard to know where his heart was.

Creative expression was an early interest, first kindled when he started taking piano and drama lessons as a young child. He did his first show at six and wrote his first song at nine. Music and performing continued to be a major focus of his life until he reached junior high school, when he first went out for sports. "I hit a snag at that point," explains Dick, "partly because I really enjoyed sports and partly because it wasn't as cool to be a musician as an athlete. So I took a detour for awhile."

Although Dick didn't give up his creative pursuits entirely—he played in the orchestra in junior high and performed in musicals in high school—he shifted his focus to athletics, an area in which he was also very gifted. By the time he got to college, he had decided to major in physical education so he could be a teacher and coach. He continued to exercise his creative gifts by playing in a country rock band and performing in musicals and plays, but it wasn't until his senior year that he realized he was on the wrong vocational track. "I started going through some massive depressive stages because I realized what I was preparing for wasn't what I wanted to do," he recalls. As a result of that realization, he pursued a scholarship to study music, which led him into the entertainment industry, where he has been working with remarkably sustained energy and enthusiasm ever since.

"I'm happiest in the right brain world," observes Dick, "and I have a difficult time in the left brain world. It's interesting because in high school I was taking advanced math and science classes and even got an award for being scientist of the year. But that seems like a lifetime ago. I now realize that what gives me the greatest joy is keeping my creative channel open."

Dick Winzeler is a talented athlete: He could have been a good coach, as he originally planned. He has a mind that is capable of comprehending the intricacies of math and chemistry and physics: He could have been a competent doctor, as his parents one time hoped. But he believes he would have been miserable if he had pursued these vocations, despite his abilities, because his passion—his gifted passion—lies in the creative arts.

Dick Winzeler is exemplary of people who love their work in that he has identified his gifted passion—which means that he knows his gifts, he knows his passions and he knows where they intersect. The same is true for most work lovers.

Knowing Your Gifts

One of the most striking characteristics of work lovers is their knowledge of their strengths and talents. When asked to reflect on their gifts, most work lovers scarcely hesitate in answering. Here are some examples:

☐ Dr. Dean Leuking, pastor: Before I ever thought of pastoral ministry, I had a sense that I could speak, that I could write and that I could lead—that I had that mysterious quality of somehow securing the confidence of other people.

☐ Kurt Neradt, dry wall taper: I'm a perfectionist, which is good, because that means the work I do ends up looking good.

☐ Greg Darnieder, director, inner-city tutoring ministry: My gifts are in taking on administrative challenges, in being able to create and grow programs in a visionary kind of way.

☐ Ken Smith (a pseudonym), CEO of a financial services firm: I guess you could say that I've got discernment and judgment. I can always make a decision and fortunately, most times, it's the right decision.

☐ Kerry Berg, mother: I'm affectionate, loving and very sensitive. Deep down inside, I always knew I'd be a good mother.

☐ Rosalie de Rosset, college professor/speaker: Public speaking is probably my greatest gift. I also have a lot of natural insight into people very quickly. That helps in teaching because I can look into the faces of my students and know what's going on emotionally, which helps me to reach out to them dimensionally.

☐ Pat Reinhofer, executive secretary: I'm very organized. I can handle a lot of responsibility and follow through on projects.

☐ Tim Botts, graphic designer/calligrapher: My greatest strength as a calligrapher is my design ability. A lot of people can do beautiful letters, but you have to know what to do with them to communicate powerfully. As a designer, I think I'm good at walking the tightrope between coming up with designs that are imaginative and yet appropriate, designs that communicate to people.

☐ Sandy Rios, singer/conductor/radio personality: My strength is communication. I'm not the best singer in the world, but I'm a good communicator and that makes my singing more effective.

☐ Elizabeth Cody Newenhuyse, author/journalist: I've been blessed with a native ability to do language—to write and to be able to read somebody else's work and, even if it's not good, be able to see the gold emerging.

☐ Chuck Swirsky, sportscaster: God gave me a tremendous mind for retention—I can tell you all kinds of information about ballplayers, who they played with, records—all that stuff. He's also given me the ability to act quickly on my feet.

☐ Telva Urban, nurse/dialysis specialist: I have an ability to do two things at once, and in my job you have to be able to do that. I can do technical procedures and talk to a patient at the same time. I can also deal with a lot of different personalities and stay easygoing.

Because they know their gifts, work lovers have a quiet confidence, a joyous certitude that they're in the right place. Consider Dr. Melicent Huneycutt, who speaks without pride, but with gentle confidence, about her gifts and how they enable her to love her ministerial vocation as pastor of spiritual life at a large midwestern church:

"I think my greatest gift is my ability to listen and really hear," she says, "that, and being able to identify with where people are, to accept them where they are, and build them up where they are. I have an ability to quietly hear, quietly receive and quietly give back.

"I also have an ability, when I study the Bible or other materials I want to teach, to hear the voice of God. I can hear something big and strong and alive. I can see how it fits into people's needs almost immediately. I'm good at giving people handles for taking hold of God.

"Another gift is the gift of waiting. Not feeling that everything has to be done today. Really perceiving that God has all of eternity to work. When I was younger I had a tendency to want to make every single thing I did superb. Successful. Tied up with pink ribbon so that everybody could see it was well done. Now I recognize that life is made up of loose ends that won't get tied up by me ever. But the ends will be tied by somebody, sometime, somewhere. My responsibility is just to live fully and completely as the person God calls me to be every day.

"I'm eloquent. Words come easily to me. I can be poetic and literary and impressive, or I can be down to earth and genuine. I have an ability to fit my words and my manner to the material at hand or the context in which something is happening."

Knowing her weaknesses is also a gift, says Melicent. "My greatest weakness is my shyness," she observes. "I thought by the time I was sixty-three I wouldn't be shy anymore. But I'm well aware that shyness is my greatest handicap in a job where extroversion is the norm. I'm the only person on the church staff who's an introvert. It's not that I'm not interested in other people, but I'm not easily self-revealing or assertive in relationships. So that's a struggle for me constantly. But because I know it's there, I can prepare myself ahead of time. *All right, we're going to brace our shoulders. Walk in with a smile. Act at ease at first and after awhile feel at ease.* It doesn't take long to be at ease when you've made up your mind about your game plan. So knowing my weaknesses is an asset to me as well as knowing my strengths."

Knowing Your Passions

People who love their work not only know their gifts, they know their passions. They know what energizes, enthuses and intrigues them. They know what it is that they can't wait to do. Listen to some work lovers talk about the work that is also their passion:

☐ Calvin Long, college math professor: "I've gotten a big kick out of doing this for the past thirty years. I do math for the same reason that artists paint. It's an art form for me. It also happens to be tremendously useful, but that's not what turns me on about it. I have to admit that I would do this even if it didn't have any utility."

☐ Dr. Peter Baker, pediatrician: It's a real joy to get up in the morning and look forward to what you're going to do that day. One of my greatest joys is holding a small child on my lap, maybe a child who was really scared of coming to the doctor's office and was crying a few minutes before, and seeing that child begin to trust me. Sometimes they'll even sort of snuggle up to me while I'm talking to them. And that's a nice feeling. I bore my wife every day with two or three stories about the neat things that have happened that day that I feel good about.

☐ David Orth, woodworker: I love the technical stuff of woodworking. I love working with tools and cutting wood and even the smells. Pulling out my hand plane is a delightful experience. I love infusing woodworking with my understanding of beauty.

☐ Melicent Huneycutt, minister: I love every part of my work except the nitpicking paperwork. I love the people work. People will come to me and say, "My life is different because you've been here." You want to say, "Yay!"

☐ Ken Phillips, psychiatrist: One of the things I love about being a psychiatrist is the fact that I can think about or apply my work in almost anything that I do. When I go to the movies, I think about life and about the emotions and struggles. When I see kids playing baseball I think, "What are they doing? They're trying to become someone, trying to please their parents, trying to find out who they are." Worship! Singing songs in worship. Becoming close to someone who is far greater than me but loves me anyway. Confession. Assurance of pardon. It's all like my work.

☐ David Himelick, carpenter/building contractor: I enjoy working with my hands and the physical activity of my job. I like the daily feeling of accomplishment, whether I'm doing the work myself or supervising the work of other people. I like organizing schedules and jobs. It can be a hassle, but I enjoy it.

☐ Rosalie de Rosset, English professor: I went to the office this weekend to prepare for a creative writing class and, as I sat there, I could just feel the excitement of that coming class hour. I thought about the time when my students would read two different magazine stories and would come back with their ideas and how much fun it would be to lead them to understand the difference between them. I can't wait for the looks of recognition and the excitement building in the students when I read them a good piece of writing and know that they're completely entranced. I absolutely love seeing students grow or feel something they haven't felt before.

☐ Kurt Neradt, dry wall taper: I like working with my hands, taking something that looks like a disaster and making it look good. I'm the kind of person who likes to go out and clean the garage—to tear everything apart and make it look really nice. That's why I love what I do.

☐ Ken Smith, CEO, financial services firm: I thrive on the competition. There's an excitement in the marketplace. You feel you're in the middle of things. I would get bored someplace where I was out of the stream of things. With a few exceptions, most mornings I'm anxious to get up and get down to work. I guess that's rare. I don't see many people with a real anticipation and enjoyment of getting into their job and getting into the fray. I'm very thankful because I've always had that.

Discovering Your Gifted Passions

You can't pursue your gifted passions if you don't know what they are. In fact, I've found that at least one of two things is usually true of people who don't enjoy their work: either they don't know their gifts or they don't know their passions. They certainly don't know their gifted passions.

If you haven't discovered your gifted passions yet, don't despair. The example and experience of work lovers interviewed for this book offer some possibilities for how to go about finding them.

Look for Clues in Your Childhood

Sometimes reflecting on your interests and accomplishments in childhood can reveal clues about your gifted passions. It's likely that both your gifts and your passions existed in embryonic form when you were very young. Illustrator Jack Stockman, for example, can hardly remember a time when he wasn't receiving recognition for his art abilities—as early as first grade, teachers and classmates were clamoring for his drawings. Author/journalist Elizabeth Cody Newenhuyse was already exhibiting signs of her inherent language abilities at age four, when she taught herself to read. Author Karen Mains says that, when she was a child, her mother never asked her what she was doing, but what she was writing. Sandy Rios was known as "the singer" in her high school by the time she was fourteen.

David Orth was always working with his hands as a child, always carving things. He carved trees, slingshots—even the front porch. Of the latter, David says ruefully, "I was so proud that I had manipulated this wood so beautifully. The first thing I did, totally innocently, was to show my dad. He wasn't real mad, but he *was* concerned about the landlord."

Chuck Swirsky was pretending to be a sportscaster as early as age five. He practiced doing play by play with baseball cards. He stood by the hour in front of station KFKF in Bellevue, Washington, watching the sports news come over the wires on a glass-encased teletype machine. He took a tape recorder to ball games and practiced his own style of sports commentary. He sat behind the closed door of his bedroom and read the sports pages from the *Seattle Times* as if he were broadcasting.

These work lovers evidenced signs of their gifted passions very early in life. It may be that you did too. Think back to your childhood and adolescence. What did you enjoy doing? What did you spend most of your free time doing? What did you do well? In reflecting on these questions, you may find clues to your current talents and passions.

Don't Be Afraid of the Trial-and-Error Method

"I discovered my gifts by the process of elimination," says church historian Martin Marty. "My wife can hear a piece of music on the radio and come over to the piano and play it. I took piano eight years and couldn't improvise two bars. I can klutz my way through a piece but it's very clear I could never be a performing musician. I reached my level of incompetence fairly early there. I love music and would probably really like to be a musician, but I'm an appreciator.

"As far as athletics are concerned—I can find my way around the tennis courts and do a few things like that. I wasn't a klutz, but I was small for the big people sports and not good at them. I remember pitching a baseball for hours thinking I was Bob Feller, who was then the hero. But when I played with other people I was at best ordinary. Why kid myself, I thought. I'll do the things I can.

"Three of my sons can build a house and I can't. I can put doorknobs on and I can parquet a floor, but I can't build a house.

"Physics, chemistry—if they give me a direction book I can follow it, but I don't have a gift for science.

"So I eliminated music, mechanics, building, sports—I could go through many, many more."

Consider the Areas in Which You Get Affirmation

One of the best ways to identify your gifts is to pay attention to those areas in which you receive the most affirmation. It probably wouldn't have occurred to Sandy Rios that she could be a professional singer, for example, had it not been for a series of affirmations from important people in her life. At age fourteen, when Sandy was convinced she was the "ugliest, fattest girl in the world," her mother insisted that she audition for a variety show—even though she was the only one Sandy would allow to hear her sing. "Sandra Kay," her mother said, "you can do it!" As things turned out, she was right—the response at the audition and later at the variety show was incredible. Throughout high school, college and after she married and had a family, Sandy continued to receive affirmation for her singing and her ability to communicate through music. Choir directors, vocal coaches, audiences and other singers all gave her the same message: You have an unusual talent and you should be using it.

Because of the way that affirmation shaped her own life, Sandy now advises others to look for similar confirmation of their talents. "I think it's really important to take cues and clues from what other people say. If you are asked to teach Sunday school and everybody says, 'Wow! That was a great job!' you might be a good teacher. And you should consider it. If you're desperate to teach, but you never get that response, you may not be in the right place. If you want to be a singer, but people aren't responding, maybe you're trying to do the wrong thing. If, on the other hand, you're getting a lot of affirmation, map out a plan and go for it."

I would add this caveat: Map out a plan and go for it, *if* the gift you've identified is compatible with your passions. Just because you *can* do something—just because you're good at it—doesn't mean you *want* to do it. Motivation makes all the difference between a gift and a gifted passion.

For many years, church music director John Folkening divided his time between teaching English, history and math at his congregation's private school and supervising the music programs at both the church and the school. John is a good teacher. But what he really loves to do is direct choirs, play the organ and develop creative worship environments through music. So for years, John loved the music director half of his job, which drew on both his passions and his gifts, and tolerated the teaching half, which drew on a set of gifts he had little natural motivation to exercise. He wanted to give up teaching entirely and devote all his time to music, but because he was good at both, his superiors were understandably reluctant to lose his talents in either area. Their view was, "If it ain't broke, don't fix it."

John was the only one who thought "it" was "broke." "When people used to affirm me for my teaching," he recalls, "instead of making me feel good, it made me think, 'What am I supposed to do, bomb in these other areas until somebody decides the only thing I'm good for is music?' You want to succeed so you wind up doing all kinds of things to the best of your ability, but in my case, it was getting in the way of what I wanted to do. The affirmation I received only added to my frustration. So affirmation alone can't be what you look to for leading."

Try Testing

Vocational tests can be very helpful in providing clues to your gifts and interests. One work lover I know says he takes a battery of vocational tests every few years to confirm his direction and find out if his gifts and interests are changing. A successful attorney I talked with recently said he decided to leave his position as general counsel of a large corporation after taking the Myers-Briggs personality test and discovering that he was more interested in short-term conceptual problem-solving than in the details of day-to-day management and departmental maintenance. Now that he's in private practice, he says, he loves almost everything about his work.

Look at the Flip Side of Your Perceived Weaknesses

It's often true that our weaknesses are also our strengths. Sometimes our weaknesses become strengths when we bring them into balance. Or when we use them in the right setting.

My husband drives me crazy with his perpetual tardiness—a function of his irrepressible optimism. He really believes that he can make it to an 11:00 worship service if he leaves home at 10:59, and we don't live next door to the church. But his unsinkable optimism is a tremendous asset to him in his role as president of a small computer company. He rides the business cycle roller coaster with very little hand-wringing because he is *convinced* that things will turn out okay. You say there's a recession going on? All the more reason businesses need to cut their costs with computers! If Paul had a job that required him to predict outcomes with a high degree of accuracy, he'd probably have a difficult time. But the same optimism that skews his judgment in some areas of life is a tremendous gift for a small business owner.

Pastor Melicent Huneycutt views her shyness as one of her greatest weaknesses, but I suspect it is also one of her greatest gifts. It gives her a point of identification with the vulnerable people she counsels. It inclines her to listen, rather than just to talk. It forces her to act intentionally, rather than just instinctively. And undoubtedly, given the fact that Melicent is gifted in so many ways, it keeps her humble—an especially attractive trait in a minister.

Give some thought to your weaknesses. Is there any way that they could be viewed as gifts?

Let Your Gifts and Passions Find You

Martin Marty didn't set out to become an internationally renowned theologian and church historian. Rather, he pursued his passions, prepared to exercise what he thought might be his gifts and then waited for them to pursue him in the form of opportunities. He explains, "I read a great deal of poetry in case I'd become a poet, which I didn't. I drew and drew and drew in case I'd become an artist, which I didn't. And I probably watched my teachers, picturing how I would teach in case I would do it, and then I did it.

"I have a strange principle in life which is based on the fact that I've never looked for things to do," he continues. "People would say, be a minister, be a field worker, be a youth worker, be a teacher, be a writer, be a student paper editor, be a minister in London, be an assistant pastor, be a graduate student. *Christian Century* magazine came and asked if I would write for them because they'd consulted at the divinity school where I attended; and the dean and two or three professors who disagreed with each other on other things agreed that I should be the one they approached. To this day, I never have yet picked an assignment. I don't know if I would have ever found anything if it hadn't found me." Kevin Miller, editor of *Christian History* magazine, was planning to go into the ministry when he began what he thought would be an interim career in editing. As a newlywed just out of college, he decided to work for a year or two and establish a financial base before he entered seminary. But in the process of doing his "interim" job, he discovered that he had a gift for writing, editing, organizing and evaluating. "I found I was more of an interior person than a social person," he explains, "that I would rather worry about the structure of an article than the structure of somebody's life crisis. I realized that the better place for me was in publishing." Today, thanks to an unintentional trial-and-error process, Kevin is an enthusiastic lover of his work—despite the fact that he had no idea what his gifted passions were when he got out of college.

Pay Attention to the Activities That Most Engage Your Focused Attention

Mihaly Csikszentmihalyi is a psychology professor at the University of Chicago. He has spent thirty years studying people who experience what he calls "flow"—the process of engaging in some work or recreational activity that is profoundly satisfying and totally absorbing. In other words, he studies people who have found their passion.

Dr. Csikszentmihalyi's research is rooted in his childhood observation that few adults seemed to enjoy their life and work. He wanted to know what parts of life people enjoyed, what makes people feel that life is worth living. In pursuit of answers to his questions, he decided to study psychology. Later, after he had started his academic career, he became fascinated by art students who would become so immersed in the process of painting that they would work for hours and sometimes days with scarcely a break for food or sleep. When they finally completed their paintings, instead of cherishing the finished project, the young artists would simply put them in a corner and start another one. Instead of seeing their completed paintings as rewards for their hard work, it seemed the students viewed them as mere excuses for doing the activity that totally engaged them.

Intrigued, Dr. Csikszentmihalyi began interviewing others who exhibited similarly intense absorption in their work or play: teachers, basketball players, surgeons, psychiatrists, chess players, long distance swimmers and many others. He found that their "flow" experiences had several characteristics in common:

They occurred when the challenges of the task at hand were balanced by the individual's skill to accomplish the task. Tennis players, for example, reported that they experienced flow when playing against an opponent whose skill level was equal to their own. When an opponent had less skill, they felt bored. When an opponent had more skill, they felt anxious. Flow only occurs when there is a balance between skill and challenge.

They occurred when an individual was able to find prompt, unam-

biguous feedback in the process of doing an activity. Dr. Csikszentmihalyi points out that surgeons tend to talk about their work as being incredibly enjoyable because they always know what they have to do and they always know if they're doing it right. Feedback is instantaneous in the operating room. Because of the feedback factor, surgeons say they wouldn't be psychiatrists for any amount of money. But psychiatrists who experience flow say they also get very clear feedback from their patients—a change in facial expression, a smile, a different tone of voice. In almost all cases, people who are experiencing flow are those who find a way to get feedback in the process of *doing* the activity that engages them.

They were characterized by an intense focusing on a task. Dr. Csikszentmihalyi's interviewees said that when they were having flow experiences, they were so focused on their task that their actions were almost automatic. They had no excess attention to think about themselves, so they performed the task without self-consciousness. All their attention was taken up by the challenge. Their focus was riveted on the present.

They were accompanied by a distorted sense of time. People who experience flow can work for hours on an activity and feel that only ten minutes have passed. Or the reverse may be true. For example, some of the dancers interviewed for Dr. Csikszentmihalyi's study reported that executing a difficult turn may take fifteen seconds in reality but feel like it takes fifteen minutes in "flow time."

People who experience flow appear to be literally energized by the activity that triggers their flow experience. According to Dr. Csikszentmihalyi, other researchers have performed follow-up studies on flow and found evidence that when people are having a flow experience their cortical activation levels drop dramatically. Normally, measures of electrical activity in the brain would go up in response to activity. But during a flow experience, there seems to be an overall saving of energy. It's important to note that, according to Dr. Csikszentmihalyi, people aren't necessarily happy during a flow experience—they're too absorbed to be aware of their own feelings. Only later, when they're reflecting on their experience, do they feel a sense of satisfaction or happiness.

Dr. Csikszentmihalyi's research points up some useful questions for people who are trying to discover their gifted passions or, to use Dr. Csikszentmihalyi's vocabulary, the activities that trigger flow experiences:

☐ What activities have I been involved with in which my skills most closely balanced the challenges of the task? (What are my gifts?)

☐ What activities give me the most clear, prompt feedback? Can I find a way to get feedback in the process of exercising my gifts?

☐ What activities engage me so completely that:

I am totally focused on the task, with little thought of the past or future?

I stop thinking about myself?

I am unaware of the passing of time or I have a distorted sense of time?

I feel energized, rather than depleted, by them?

If there is an activity or group of activities that show up as answers to most or all of these questions, you probably have a gifted passion. You can confirm the existence of a gifted passion by looking for clues in your childhood interests, by paying attention to areas in which you consistently receive affirmation and by using the trial-and-error method of discovery. Follow your interests and then see if the results not only point to the existence of a gift, but also demonstrate that your interest is sustained over a period of time.

If you have a gifted passion, God created you to use it. See if you can find a way to make a living exercising it.

4

Process Versus Goals: Finding Feedback

I like reaching goals, but once I do,
I try to find another process.
ELIZABETH CODY NEWENHUYSE,
AUTHOR/JOURNALIST

AFTER COMPLETING THE FIRST FEW INTERVIEWS FOR THIS BOOK, I WAS becoming convinced that work lovers are for the most part process-oriented folks who derive more satisfaction from doing their work than reflecting on results. I came to that conclusion after hearing a lot of comments like these:

☐ Dick Winzeler, writer/musician/actor: I believe that what's important is not the product, but the process. But our culture is all about product. We don't ask an athlete how it felt to run down a field or swim down a lane. We ask, how does it feel to win? But there are a lot of people who have gotten positive feedback in the form of commercial success who are still unhappy because they feel torture in the process.

☐ Karen Mains, author: What gives me the greatest pleasure is the process of my work. I'm surprised that there are people who find it meaningful, but that also feeds and gives meaning to the process. I don't think about the reception when I'm writing, I just think about doing the best job I can do. I think I could be happy if I had never found a publisher or had a readership. The public thing doesn't drive me at all.

☐ Peter Baker, pediatrician: I think the process has to be fun. I invested eight years of training to get into this direction and I enjoyed that time—the discipline, the study, the association with people. It was a rich time. Not every moment was fun, but the process was fun. I think that's the only way to do it. You either have to have this overriding notion that you'll make a lot of money and it'll get better later, or you've got to enjoy the process. I think the healthier way to go is to enjoy the process.

☐ Melicent Huneycutt, pastor: I love the process. I love preparing a sermon just as much as I do preaching. And I love preaching the sermon as much as I do the encouragement that comes back to me. I love studying for a teaching time. Developing a course. Ordering the concepts so that one flows out of the next. Thinking of illustrations that bring them to life. That's just fun. But so are the actual teaching and interacting with people. I like every part of my work.

Work lovers, I concluded from comments such as these, are people who have found a way to make a living from a process they enjoy. But then I started encountering avid work lovers who confessed that it wasn't so much the process of their work they enjoyed—but achieving goals.

"I find satisfaction in my work whenever I make any kind of breakthrough or overcome an obstacle," says prison ministry executive Ron Nikkel. "I love being able to convince difficult prison officials to let us into an institution, or being able to get a hearing from a difficult group of inmates. So for me, joy in work comes not so much from the process but from reaching a goal."

Then there's college president David Horner: "My pleasure

comes mainly from a sense of accomplishment," he says. "I get really frustrated if things aren't pulled off the way I think they were supposed to be, so my pleasure or displeasure is pretty much tied to results."

Are these goal-directed people exceptions? Or is it the other way around? Or is process versus goal orientation simply not a factor in loving your work?

I got a clue about the answer to these questions when I attended a lecture by University of Chicago researcher Mihaly Csikszentmihalyi. Dr. Csikszentmihalyi, as you may recall, has spent many years studying a phenomenon he calls "flow"—the process of engaging in some work or recreational activity that is tremendously satisfying and totally absorbing. Dr. Csikszentmihalyi observed that one of the characteristics of a flow experience is "prompt, unambiguous feedback."

It's not clear that all work lovers experience "flow" as Dr. Csikszentmihalyi defines it. But as I reflect on the work lovers I've talked to, it occurs to me that most of them are able to get some kind of satisfying feedback—an immediate sense of pleasure or a clear response which lets them know how well they're doing—from their work. For some, the feedback occurs in the very process of doing the work. For others, the feedback comes from the results of their work.

For graphic designer Tim Botts, the process *is* the feedback. Tim appreciates the lavish praise he receives for many of his calligraphy and book designs, but he doesn't think he could love his work as much if the process were different—even if the results were the same. "For me, there's joy in every step along the way," he says. "The fact that I love the process so much is the reason I haven't jumped in to use the computer. I've had training to do it, but it's still not for me because it's just not as much fun as the tactile, hands-on, pencil-on-paper work that I do."

Chiropractor Robert Gross works with people, not pencil and paper. For him, the feedback in his work comes not only from seeing patients feel better, but from touching them with healing hands. "When I put my hands on my patients," he says, "I get as much back from them as I give. When I was in training, I used to follow other chiropractors in their offices. I'd go from room to room with them and, after two hours, I was drained. But they would be as refreshed as the minute they started—because you get something back from a person when you touch them."

David Horner says that, despite his strong goal-directedness, he is also able to derive feedback from the activities that make up his work. "We have a place up in Maine," he says, "and sometimes I'll go up there and just sit on the rocks and think, 'What if we spin the curriculum this way?' or 'What if we did this with the faculty lineup?' A lot of these ideas I've never proposed to anybody—I just like playing with problems that way. So there's a creative and imaginative process that goes on in my work that is its own reward."

Whether it comes from the process, from the results or both, work lovers clearly seem to be able to get feedback from their work:

☐ Dave Himelick, carpenter/contractor: I like the daily feeling of accomplishment in my work. That's something that's real important to me. One of the things that was really frustrating to me in my job at the University, which was real research-oriented, was the fact that I might or might not see any results. I guess I need that on a daily basis.

☐ David Hogue, pastoral counselor: I've had cases where it's felt like a privilege to be there when a breakthrough happened. It feels like what I imagine a midwife feels and that's incredibly powerful. Sometimes it feels very rare, but when it happens, it helps me remember during the long periods when nothing seems to be happening.

☐ Rosalie de Rosset, English professor: When I go to give a

lecture on one of the great novels and I know how much it has changed me, I cannot wait for the looks of recognition, the excitement in my students. How can I describe what it feels like to read them a good piece of writing and know that they're completely entranced? I absolutely love seeing somebody grow or feel something they haven't felt before.

It doesn't seem to matter whether you're process-oriented or goal-directed. If you can find a way to get feedback from your work, you're more likely to enjoy it than if you don't get feedback, or the kind of feedback you want. Because there's nothing like giving yourself wholeheartedly to a task and getting a clear message back: "This is fun. This is important. This is beautiful. This is effective." Just ask tutoring ministry director Greg Darnieder:

"My satisfaction basically centers around the growth and accomplishments of the people we work with," he says. "I think of one of our girls—the shyest, mousiest young lady you ever set your eyes on. She went to two different junior colleges and didn't make it because she just wasn't self-disciplined enough. She is just tremendous with kids—she has the gifts to be a teacher—but having come through the city's public school system, she didn't have a strong enough background to succeed. So when she got in trouble at junior college, she came to us to figure out what the next best thing was. She thought that maybe she could become a classroom assistant. After spending two years with us, she found another school where she basically started over. Now she has a B average and she's majoring in elementary education. She told me last week, 'I've decided I'm going to become a teacher.' She has a vision now that's achievable. It's been tremendously satisfying to have been part of her life for two years and to see her growth and her willingness not to give up on herself. That's really neat. Really neat. And tomorrow that process continues."

Feedback. Some people find it in processes. Some people find

it in results. If you can figure out what kind of feedback you need—
and where you're most likely to get it—you'll have taken a big step
toward finding work you can love.

5

Risk-Taking: Stepping Out in Faith

---

*Being able to feel joy involves risk-taking, and I do not mean
juggling monies around frenziedly in the stock market.
It means risking your popularity by taking a genuinely unpopular stand,
risking your life to do what it is that YOU want to do in life. Risks are
going to be there anyway. It's just street sense to take them on your
terms, not theirs. In warfare, it is called being on the offensive. In life,
it is called embracing life with all your heart.*

**GEORGIE ANNE GEYER,
NEWSPAPER CORRESPONDENT**

---

*By faith Abraham, when called to go to a place he would
later receive as his inheritance, obeyed and went, even
though he did not know where he was going.*

HEBREWS 11:8

"I'VE GOT A PAYROLL IN TWO DAYS OF ALMOST $40,000," SAYS GREG DAR-
nieder quietly, sitting in his modest office on Chicago's Near North
Side. "I've got $15,000 right now. I have to pay people in forty-eight
hours, and I'm not sure where the rest of the money is going to
come from.

"We've taken a lot of risks. This one payroll is almost twice as
much as my budget for the whole first year this organization was

in existence. We've said, 'This program is important' and 'This aspect is important,' and it'll all work out. Sometimes it gets real scary, and I've gone a couple of times myself without getting paid, but we've never missed a payroll.

"Ninety-nine per cent of our support comes from donations. We rely on lots of people, lots of organizations and lots of churches. But there's a real sense of dependence on God's provision."

Greg Darnieder, executive director of CYCLE, a not-for-profit educational organization serving kids from one of Chicago's poorest neighborhood, is a risk-taker. As such, he is exemplary of almost all the work lovers interviewed for this book.

In listening to the stories of people who love their work, I found that most of them were, at some level, stories of risk. Which is not to say that all work lovers are risk-takers by nature. Far from it.

I think of my own father, an extremely conservative and cautious man, who at age thirty-six left a secure position with a bank in Oregon to move to the Midwest in search of "full-time Christian work." His wife, my mother, was six months pregnant with their third child, he had no specific prospects, and all their friends and family members thought he had lost his mind. But within a few weeks he was employed by Moody Bible Institute, where he thrived for the next thirty-two years until his retirement.

My father's behavior in this situation—which others viewed as foolhardy and he viewed as stepping out in faith—was completely uncharacteristic of him. But it led him directly, against all odds, to the work he ended up loving for more than three decades.

Many of the work lovers I interviewed were like my father: they took risks despite their naturally cautious dispositions. Others were born risk-takers who loved the thrill of being on the edge. Some took risks to find their vocation. Others took—and continue taking—risks in the very doing of their work.

The risks that work lovers take may be emotional or financial or even unconscious. But more often than not, people who love their work *do* take risks. Even if they are not characteristically risk-takers, most say they have taken a significant vocational leap of faith at some point in their journey.

Psychiatrist Ken Phillips is among those who took a risk to pursue the profession they now love. Ken grew up in a religious environment that viewed psychology and psychiatry as worldly. The feeling among many people he knew was, if you're really spiritual, you'll take your problems to God. So when he broke the news of his choice of vocations, it was quite a bombshell. "The biggest risk I've ever taken was telling my family and the whole culture and milieu I came from that I was going to do something they considered quite radical," recalls Ken. "The reaction was, 'Here's our oldest son, the first person in our family to go to college, a real bright boy in the church. What's he throwing his life away for? Why is he doing that? We thought he was going to become someone important!' "

Because of the attitudes he grew up with, Ken agonized before making his decision to pursue psychiatry. In medical school, he considered ophthalmology, family practice—almost every specialty except psychiatry—but found they held no interest for him. He even took a year off after medical school, taking the highly unusual step of postponing his specialty training until he could figure out what he wanted to do with his life. After many months of soul-searching and struggling with despair he finally decided to pursue his dream of practicing psychiatry. Although it felt extremely risky at the time, Ken says his only regret now is that he didn't make the decision earlier. "I could have saved myself some time and a major depression if I'd only allowed myself to follow my dream a little sooner," he says.

Harold Myra was thirty-five years old and the editor of *Campus Life* magazine when he took on the risk-laden challenge that opened up whole new horizons in his work life: he said yes when the decision-makers at *Christianity Today* magazine asked him to head up the Christianity Today organization as publisher and chief executive officer.

"I still remember going out to Washington, D.C., where *Christianity Today* was located at the time," says Harold. "Here I was, this *Campus Life* guy, being asked to take over this intellectual, scholarly organization and move it to Atlanta or Chicago. There was some question whether the company could even survive because of the financial problems they were having. My wife was pregnant with our third child. But I still went ahead and took a job that might not turn out to be a job. And I found it all so exciting that I didn't sleep that entire night, which is unlike me."

The risk paid off for Harold, who has not only retained his job as publisher and president of Christianity Today, Inc., but has guided the company to financial strength and editorial dominance in the field of Christian magazine publishing.

"In some ways I'm pretty conservative," says Harold, "but when there is a big risk to be taken, I find that kind of fun. It pumps my adrenaline."

While some work lovers have taken risks to pursue their vocational dreams, others choose risk in the work they already have— even though they could easily play it safe. Marlene LeFever is a manager with the David C. Cook company, a well-known publisher of Christian education materials. Given her stature and tenure in the company, Marlene could easily coast on some of her past accomplishments. But she refuses to do that, despite the fact that the prospect of failure looms larger in proportion to her success.

"The older I get and the more people come to me," she explains, "the more difficult it is to take risks—because I have more to lose. When I wrote an article that bombed twenty years ago, that wasn't so awful. If I write an article that bombs today, that is being published in a magazine that lots of people could benefit from and I miss that opportunity, that's a little more devastating. So it becomes a caution for me to stay creative. But you can't stay creative without taking risks. And you can't take risks without failing.

"When my friend Joe Bayly, who died a couple of years ago, was president of this company, he and I used to go to each other with the question 'What are you doing this year that you know you can't accomplish without God's help?'

"It's so easy to take only the assignments I know I can do, and not the ones that go a step further and say, I am really on the edge here. I've either got to pull in everything I've got and become more creative or I'm not going to pull this off. That's sort of the challenge for me to take on things that will allow me to fail—not projects that are structured to fail, but projects that have the potential for failure."

When I think about risk-taking in the very doing of one's job, I think of a graphic designer for another well-known publishing company. Each week he meets with a decision-making committee to present book cover concepts. In his early years with the company, the committee frequently gave a thumbs down to his designs, which they often felt were too modern and unconventional. But he persisted in taking creative risks. "Taking risks is very important to me in my creative work," he says, "even though it would probably make my job easier if I gave the committee what they wanted every week. But I've always given them what I believe is the best I can do, even when I knew they wouldn't like it because it was too new for them. As an artist of integrity, I feel I have to do that. I have to play a teaching role. Sometimes they would surprise me and approve something I didn't think they would. And now, it's a totally new day. That tells me it's better to take risks than to be really conservative as an artist."

Although some work lovers choose to take risks in their work, others choose work in which risk is inherent. Chuck Swirsky is a sportscaster for WGN, the top-rated radio station in Chicago. In choosing to be a sportscaster, he says, he is choosing risk on a daily basis.

"I enjoy this business," he says. "I get excited about it, I love it and, when I come in to work, I'm on fire. But I know I'm going to get fired. It's like being a manager for a sports team. The moment a manager is hired, the clock starts ticking. It's just a matter of time before he's going to get it. For some guys, it might be a year and a half. For others, it might be eleven years. Sooner or later, unless I leave, WGN is going to come to me and say, 'You've had a great run here. We appreciate it. But we're going to make a move.' Boom, they give you your two weeks' pay and you're outta there.

"I used to have a big problem with that, because I thought that was no way to live. But in this business, you live on the edge. And the reality is, there's risk in everything. You can't be attached to a certain part of your world and find your security there. There *is* no security except knowing that Christ is in your heart."

Few people would suspect how acutely Martin Marty perceives the risk he says is inherent in preaching. Despite international renown, he says he still suffers an attack of nerves whenever he is called upon to preach—even if he's only giving a chapel talk to eighteen people. "I had breakfast with my son prior to preaching at his church a couple of years ago and afterwards he said, 'Dad, why were you so nervous this morning? You've been preaching and speaking for forty years. Why are you nervous now?' I said, 'I'm much more nervous preaching than speaking. Pick anybody you like out of a congregation. She might be addicted to something. She might be ill. She might be giving church its only chance in years. She might think she's going to hear someone else and instead she gets me. I might win nine out of ten people, but lose the tenth.'

"I was backstage once with a great violinist and somebody said,

'You know the reviews will be good. Why are you nervous?' And he said, 'Well, for me, it's the 3,000th time; this is their only night." I always think of that when I see a preacher who is casual. The risk of turning casual is horrible."

Some work lovers take risks, as my dad did, without any safety net. Others take considered risks. I think of Jim Steere, for example, who gave up a lucrative career as a jeweler to pursue his dream of becoming a professional photographer. "Although leaving the jewelry business was an act of faith," he explains, "I had an opportunity to ease into it. I talked to my father-in-law (who owned the store and was planning to turn the business over to Jim) about leaving the store and even asked if we could set up an arrangement where I worked at the store part-time for a year while I worked on setting up my own business. So even though I gave up something that was relatively secure, I had a chance to test the waters pretty thoroughly before I made the move."

Some people who love their work say they take risks reluctantly, while others ruefully admit to being risk-takers by nature.

Pastoral counselor David Hogue is among the former. "I'm a pretty cautious person," he says. "It takes me a long time to get around to taking risks, and even then it's a pretty measured risk." Measured or not, Hogue does take risks. He left a secure job as a hospital chaplain and uprooted his family to pursue a graduate degree in counseling. And he started a church-based counseling center with only a small percentage chance that it could be a success. "All my training said that the kind of long-term, intensive counseling I was trained to do couldn't happen in a parish setting," observes Hogue. "Supposedly, it had to be done in a place where you didn't have any other contact with the clients. So when they asked me to start the center, I had to say, 'I don't know if it will work, but I'll try it.' And I did it and it worked."

Marlene LeFever is another reluctant risk-taker. "I'm not an automatic risk-taker," says Marlene. "I've never gone up in a hot air balloon or jumped out of an airplane. I take risks because I know it is absolutely imperative if I'm going to continue to be used by God. The only way I'm going to continue to grow is to take what for me would be a risk."

Rosalie de Rosset, who as a "very insecure, afraid young girl" left a small town to come to work at a radio station in Chicago and later became a college English teacher in the same city, describes her experience similarly. "I'm not the risk-taking type, but I've taken tremendous risks," she observes. "It's been the grace of God that has pushed me. Sometimes I take risks out of desperation—when nothing is working, I'll do it. I don't like it, but I take risks anyway."

Free-lance illustrator Jack Stockman exemplifies the other kind of risk-taker. "God gave me a risk-taking, gregarious personality," he says, "which is good because probably eighty per cent of my occupation depends on selling. I know hundreds of people who really have an ability at art, and several people who've come to me for advice about getting into the business, but I can tell they'll probably never get into it as an occupation because they're not able to risk to the extent that risk needs to be taken, or they don't have ability to sell their product."

Many of the work lovers I talked to are like Jack in that they are natural risk-takers—and they're well aware of their risk-taking tendencies. Consider:

☐ David Orth, woodworker: I'm a gambler by nature. As a small-business person, I'm out there every day looking for a job. I get hired every day. I take risks every day. I will always gamble for something I think is worth doing.

☐ Richard Blackburn, high-school English teacher: I'm a gambler. I know that about myself. That's why I rejected the tedium of a nine-to-five business job. I think a lot of people in the corporate world have missed out on cosmic risk-taking.

☐ Karen Mains, author: I like risky things. I like dangerous circumstances. I was in Beirut in 1982 and if someone would call today and say, "Karen, there's an assignment in Beirut," I would go. So I guess it's part of my nature to love risk.

Some work lovers are such natural risk-takers that they run their risks unconsciously—only recognizing them in retrospect. David Horner, president of North Park College, is among them. David is a tall man with dark curly hair and an aura of purposefulness. He's has been taking risks most of his adult life—turning his back on a successful family business in order to study philosophy, borrowing half a million dollars to start a tennis club at age twenty-one, accepting the presidency of a small eastern college at age twenty-nine.

"I have a strong ability to run risks but, often, I'm not even aware of them," admits David. "I have a son who's twenty-one now and if he came in and asked for half a million dollars to do a business venture, I'm sure I wouldn't give it to him. He doesn't know enough. But I did those kinds of things and they were risky, often more risky than I knew."

Even when he's aware of the hazards, David is willing to risk. "I don't even think that much about risk or political consequences," he muses. "I just think about what's right to do, what would be good."

That's why he didn't even consider the risks when, at age thirty-four, he merged himself out of a job. "I was president of a small college," David explains, "and I made a decision to merge it with a similar institution. The school I headed was my alma mater, but I merged it out of existence. A lot of people have said to me, 'I never would have done that. I would have gotten out of there. I would have done something, but I wouldn't have done that.' But to me, it seemed like the right thing to do to produce the best education for the students—which was our mission. I didn't think that much about the political consequences."

The political consequences were clear: he was going to be out of a job. But today, after a brief stint in the corporate world, David Horner is once again a college president who loves his work.

Work lovers not only differ in the way they take risks, they differ in what they put at risk. For some, it's money. For others, it's emotional security. For still others, it's reputation.

Singer Sandy Rios put her financial future at risk to produce her first album. "Making albums is expensive," she says. "I've had to stick my neck way out. Sometimes I get discouraged and think, 'I can't do this anymore. I can't put my children in this position. I've just got to quit and get a real job, a teaching job or something.' And then I'll have all these encouragements. So I think risk is important. Not foolish risk or selfish risk. But risk is important."

High-school vocational counselor Judy Everswick puts her emotions on the line every day in her work with teen-agers. "When you're building relationships with other people, you have to be vulnerable," she explains. "So I'm vulnerable."

Author Karen Mains is putting the affection and good will of her loyal readers—who have come to love her for ministry-oriented religious books—at risk with her newest writing project. "It's a pot-boiler novel," she says. "One subtext is like a contemporary *Scarlet Letter*. It's a beautiful picture of God's redemptive grace in the lives of fallen people. But there's no evangelical publishing house that will touch it."

Martin Marty has put, and is putting, his reputation, his character and his comfort at risk. "One's whole life, when you're in the Christianity-imparting, opinion-forming business, can be shattered by one false move," he explains. "There could be that one move that demonstrates an absence of integrity, that is very near the edge of what looks like integrity. And I'm not sure any of us knows quite where that line is.

"Then there are other risks," he continues. "Consider a not-very-representative side of life—the Selma march. I had a call from Dr. King's organization and produced a handful of people and we went down there and marched and came home. There was a physical risk. I was scared. I was scared for life and limb. There wasn't a big moral risk. After all, the *Christian Century* says, 'We stand for things like that.' The University of Chicago says, 'That's what we stand for.' If I'd been a pastor, as I was a year earlier, I'd have had a different kind of risk. I'd have had to go back and explain to 800 people what I was doing down there.

"But now I have the risk of getting ego satisfaction from it. I can show you my picture at Selma in an old *Life* magazine. They weren't intending to take my photo, but there I was. I was out of character that day. I was doing what that day demanded, but I'm not a demonstrator. I don't want to be a Dan Berrigan who demonstrates, demonstrates, demonstrates. Because if you keep talking to the converted, you stop doing what you're supposed to do. So one of my risks is letting out-of-character actions become part of character.

"I think one of the biggest risks in the teaching profession is not flunking somebody you should flunk. One of my teachers had a saying on his desk that I've memorized: 'God give me the courage to flunk my best student.'

"I think there's a risk of coasting. I have a discipline of telling everyone who writes to me asking me to speak: 'Please assign a topic.' I also have an obsession to preach the biblical text of the week. I have five cabinets full of notes from old lectures that I could easily rely on, but I have a horror of letting myself fall into the habit of dipping in. I have a horror of repeating myself.

"But the biggest risk," concludes the respected university professor, "is violating the covenant with the student, or the reader, or the audience. There's a covenant with them that one can use or misuse."

Work lovers take risks. Some are natural risk-takers, people who love to live on the edge, who love to stare danger in the face and make it blink. Many work lovers, however, are cautious folks who somehow found the courage to risk and found to their relief that it paid off.

Some work lovers have taken thumping risks. Risks that, viewed logically, never should have been taken. But somehow, God honored what were often tremendous leaps of faith. My father, for example, thinks that may be true of the risk he took in leaving his job at the bank.

"I think it's possible that it was a foolhardy thing to do and the Lord honored my motives anyway," he muses. "I wouldn't necessarily recommend what I did to someone else. Normally, I think it's better to get another job before you leave the old one. But I had the conviction that the Lord wanted me in full-time Christian work, and so I went from there.

"I think what God called Abraham to do—to go out without knowing where he was going—is a bit unusual. It was outside of the norm. I feel the same way about what I did. It isn't what God expects all the time. But there are times when he expects you to step out in faith."

People who love their work are people who are willing to risk. Sometimes they risk eagerly, sometimes reluctantly. But risk they do. When they believe they have heard the voice of God, they step out in faith. Like Abraham, when they're called, they obey—even when they don't know where they're going.

6

Making Sacrifices

The most important question to ask about a job isn't,
"What does it pay?" but "What does it cost?"

DAVID BLOOM,
JAZZ MUSICIAN

Getting a Ph.D. was inordinately hard. I worked from eight in the
morning to eleven at night, six days a week and half a day on
Sunday. When I talked to one of my teachers about my situation,
he said, "Mr. Long, I don't know many people who get
a Ph.D. unless they want it rather badly."

CALVIN LONG,
MATH PROFESSOR

IT'S SURPRISING, AT LEAST TO ME, HOW MANY WORK LOVERS SAY THAT
sacrifice is not part of their story. Unlike Calvin Long, many people
apparently are able to pursue the work they love without feeling
that they are working "inordinately" hard or giving up leisure time
or money or family life. Take Martin Marty, for example. The
church historian says that, while sacrifice is part of his Christian
life, it hasn't been a big part of his work.

"I've had such a fortunate life," he says. "I sacrificed parish
ministry to go into full-time teaching, but the teaching was so over-
whelmingly rewarding that I could never look back and call it
sacrifice. I don't think I sacrificed family life for work. I don't think
I sacrificed spousal love. I was the only person in the neighbor-

hood who tossed a football with kids after school. I controlled my schedule, and it would have been my fault if I didn't. When you're in a law firm and they're making demands, you're not that free. We didn't make financial sacrifices. Money eventually came to me more easily than it does to most profs in my field. I don't make a sacrifice of intellect for the sake of the faith. I don't sneak around the campus thinking, 'Oh, they'll think less of me because I'm a believer or I am less of a believer.' It just seems to me that the Christian faith opens one to more, not less. So I can't say that sacrifice has been part of my work story."

Martin Marty's experience is similar to that of many work lovers. But not all of them. Sacrifice is a theme in the lives of enough people who love their work that to ignore their stories would be to present an incomplete picture.

Alice Rubash didn't necessarily choose to sacrifice, but she says the sacrifices she ended up making have created qualities in her that enable her to pursue the work she loves today. Her role as volunteer director of her congregation's Stephen Ministry requires a deep understanding of people who are hurting and lonely, people who ache with the pain of loss.

As the wife of a much-transferred oil executive, Alice knows what it feels like to be lonely. To be, yet again, the stranger in a new community. To feel with every nerve ending the loss of friends and home and familiarity.

Alice has lived all over the world. She can scarcely count the number of times she's heard the words, "Darling, we're transferred." And packed boxes. And looked for a new house and school and church. And a new set of friends.

"I remember meeting a woman when we first moved to Calgary," Alice recalls. "I knew she would be a good friend eventually, but as I drove away from her home I started crying, thinking, 'I don't want this new friend. I want my old friends who know me.' The same thing happened when we moved here. When we joined the church the pastor said, 'Mr. and Mrs. Rubash come to us from Canada where they belonged to the such-and-such church.' And the tears started coming down my face and I thought, 'I don't want this church. I want my old church where they loved me and I knew them and we cared about each other and I had a place.'

"I remember when we'd moved again and the kids were all gone and Norm was gone half the time and I was so lonely. I went to a women's meeting and I met the president of the group, and I said, 'You know, I've just moved here from Egypt—I'm new in the community.' And she said, 'Oh, you've just moved from Egypt.' And she turned to someone else and that was it. She didn't know what else to say or do with me. I remember getting very angry and thinking, 'Isn't there anyone here who sees that there's a stranger?' That experience has stood me in good stead because I now know how strangers feel. I know what it feels like to be on the outside.

"I think I had to go through that to get to where I am," she reflects. "It made me sensitive to other people when they are in a place of loss. My sacrifices haven't been sacrifices of choice, but they've made me a different person and I like the person I've become. I've learned to be myself and to find the places I can do my work wherever I am."

Psychiatrist Ken Phillips has a different story. He had to make significant sacrifices to get to where he is, but his sacrifices were clearly chosen. For years, he chose to give up possessions, a social life, virtually all his free time—in pursuit of a career in medicine.

Medical school and residency were very, very hard, he says. He worked seven days a week. His friends were graduating from college and buying cars and getting jobs and he was borrowing money for still more years of arduous schooling. "I was cleaning bed pans and standing for ten hours holding retractors on someone who was having a belly operation and thinking, 'This is nothing related to what I want to do with my life whatsoever,' " says Ken. "Studying till one in the morning, memorizing hundreds and thousands of picky little details about nerves and muscles that I was going to regurgitate on an exam and then forget as soon as I was done. I kept asking myself, 'What's the meaning of all this, besides getting into the club?'

"I'm so fulfilled right now that I almost feel guilty complaining about the dues I had to pay. But at the time, it was quite crushing."

Ken Phillips is glad to look *back* on his period of sacrifice. But writer/publishing executive Marlene LeFever says sacrifice continues to be part of her story: "I haven't had to sacrifice money since I left the mission field," she says, "but I have had to sacrifice time. Everyone else enjoys summer and I'm in here trying desperately to write an article on the love of God, or the next book my husband seems to think I need to write. My days are usually very, very long. I work on material for the company until late in the afternoon and then on writing till late in the evening, because I love to write.

"I've made sacrifices in my marriage. I don't have children. If I did, I wouldn't be able to do what I do. And I'm willing to sometimes miss having supper with my husband. Willing to work weekends. So in a way, my husband is sacrificing too.

"There's been a sacrifice of options. When you decide on a career path, you close doors. And that's not bad. But I will never be some of the things I might have been if I'd taken a different path. I do have some of the talent, for example, that would allow me to be a fairly competent artist. But I will never be an artist, although I'll always draw little pictures, because I've chosen to be a writer. And that hurts, every time I close a door. Every time I have to say, 'No, that's not me, I can't do that,' I feel a little dying. But again, like everything, there's also an affirmation of the direction I've chosen to go.

"I've sacrificed secrecy of selfhood," she continues. "When I write, I tend to give away more about myself than I want to, and yet I know I can't make the impact if I don't share the guts. So I give up privacy and personhood. The Amish people believe that if you take their picture, you're stealing part of who they are. In a way, it's like that for me as a Christian writer. If you take my picture, you take my soul. It's not theologically true, of course, but in my writing, I'll share a picture of my soul even if I have to clean up the blood afterwards. If it's valuable to what I'm doing, I'm willing. And there's a loss in that."

Pastor and former missionary Melicent Huneycutt admits to having sacrificed to pursue her vocation but, like many work lovers, says it rarely felt like sacrifice. Although she worked two or sometimes three jobs at a time to put herself through school, for example, she found she used the skills she developed many times over in a later life. She gave up a lot of material comfort to work as a missionary in post-war Korea, but she scarcely noticed what she was missing. "It didn't feel like a sacrifice because I filled my house with little children who didn't have anyone to care for them and I got their love and enthusiasm in return," she says. "I never came home to a cold, empty apartment as so many young career women say they do. I'd see all these little eyes pressed to the window waiting for me to come home, thrilled when I came in the door. So there was a lot of affirmation and joy in what I was doing."

She's sacrificed financially—as she looks toward retirement she realizes she's going to be living on social security and not much else—but she doesn't have any regrets. "I've never really felt the pinch of not having any money," she says, "even as a missionary, when I was only being paid $145 a month. When I was caring for all those little children, our diets were restricted, but we had a good time. There was one day a week, for example, that each child would get an egg. Egg day was like a birthday. We celebrated your egg.

So it's really hard to say that I've felt sacrifice.

"Perhaps I have felt the sacrifice of freedom," she admits. "When you're in a very public role, your actions are watched and commented on by a lot of people. That I've sensed as the greatest sacrifice of all—the goldfish bowl complex does come in. I don't know of a good side to that one. But all the other sacrifices were really balanced with something I got in return."

Just because sacrifice is balanced by something in return doesn't mean it doesn't pinch. Full-time mother Ann Anderson is glad she sacrificed her planned career as a historian instead of sacrificing the opportunity to raise her children, but she's aware—sometimes acutely—of what she gave up. "When I gave up the career I'd planned and worked on and hoped for, I gave up the status that went with it," she says. "I remember when I was working on a committee for a volunteer cause and when I offered to do something one woman said, 'Oh, yes, let Ann do it because every day is a day off for her.' I like this person and I know she didn't mean it in a malicious way at all but, from her perspective, that's what my life is. I don't feel that I'm constantly battling negative images of the housewife, but I do notice them. So I've sacrificed a certain image in the eyes of people who do make money. But it's the lesser of two sacrifices."

One of the most frequent sacrifices cited by work lovers is a sacrifice of money. Many work lovers have consciously chosen modest-paying vocations over more lucrative but less satisfying work. But having chosen, they sometimes continue to feel their sacrifices.

"Sometimes I get depressed when I look at my income figures and realize my younger brothers were doing this well ten years ago," says woodworker David Orth. "My brothers were buying houses right out of college, and I'm still renting an apartment and driving a rust-bucket car. But as an article in *Business Week* pointed out, even though making high-end furniture is becoming a big thing—some pieces are selling for $20,000 and up—the problem of getting here is that people aren't willing to live on the poverty level for five to ten years. So I've put making money on the back burner. I think it has to be like that if you're going to follow your bliss.

"I feel basically successful, but I also know how close I've come to failure. And I know I'm always just this close to failure. Sometimes I wish I could get rid of that fear, and sometimes I wonder if it doesn't make the whole thing more valuable."

Money is only one of the sacrifices that work lovers make:

☐ Karen Mains, author: In order to write and raise children and be in the ministry, I haven't had a lot of time for socializing. There hasn't been time for ladies' luncheons. I used to enjoy stripping furniture and going to the Art Institute, but recently I haven't had time for that either. And there have been sacrifices in friendship. Even to be my friend takes a lot of understanding because, when I'm writing, I'm not there, or I'm not there very well. And I'll be involved for four, five or six months on a project. So there have been some enormous sacrifices.

☐ Gary Ginter, businessman: I worked a lot of seventy- and eighty-hour weeks early in my career. I certainly sacrificed by being away from my family about forty per cent of the time for several years. And I sacrificed part of my personal agenda by never finishing my degree. I may be the only Phi Beta Kappa who never got his B.A.

☐ Kevin Miller, magazine editor: One thing I've sacrificed is the amount of free-lance writing I do. I'd like to do more, but I can't dissipate my energies for that. I want to do a good job when I'm here. I want to be on top of my game, and I can't do that when I'm constantly doing other things outside. I say no to a lot of assignments, and it's painful because most of them are interesting to me.

Not all work lovers sacrifice to pursue their vocations. Many say sacrifice isn't part of their story at all. Others acknowledge having made what others might consider sacrifices, but say they never really felt them.

But sacrifice, whether chosen or unchosen, is a theme in the lives of enough work lovers to warrant a couple of observations. If you want to pursue work you can love, be prepared for the possibility that you may have to sacrifice—time, money, options, comfort, security, prestige—along the way. If you're sacrificing right now and don't see any light at the end of the tunnel, remember the stories of Alice Rubash and Ken Phillips and Calvin Long and Marlene LeFever. These and many other work lovers say their past and present sacrifices are well worth making. Because for them, not being able to love their work would be a much greater sacrifice.

7

Developing Competence

I couldn't love what I do if I didn't think I was good at it.
DAVID HORNER,
COLLEGE PRESIDENT

PEOPLE WHO LOVE THEIR WORK ARE PEOPLE WHO ARE COMPETENT AT what they do. Being competent, of course, is not the same as being gifted. I had an acquaintance in college, for example, who was probably one of the most naturally gifted singers I've ever met. His vocal teachers agreed that, with his extraordinary tenor voice and striking good looks, he had the potential to become a major opera star. And yet he gave one of the most incompetent senior recitals I've ever been embarrassed to witness. He bumbled his way through the concert, stumbling over the words to some songs, humming his way through others—not because of excessive nerves, but because he lacked the discipline to practice and memorize his music.

Competence usually requires some degree of giftedness, but it also requires diligence and work and time.

Ann Anderson has reached the point where she is confident of her competence as a full-time mother, but she didn't always feel that way. For the first six months of her son's life—when he was barely eating and rarely sleeping—she seriously questioned whether she was suited to be a parent. "Those first few months were really a shock to me," she recalls. "I really felt like I was the problem, that I was being obsessive and not having the right approach at all." Ann's response to her own perceived incompetence: she read every parenting book she could get her hands on and she didn't give up. Now the mother of two children, she finds herself being looked to as a role model by other parents.

Ann can take comfort in the fact that, while it took her six months to develop a sense of competence in her work, it often takes others much longer. Ken Phillips, for example, says it took him five years to feel competent as a psychiatrist. "After twelve years of school, they were turning me loose and I still felt totally incompetent," he says in retrospect. "I took a job in another state with a senior psychiatrist and we were trying to decide how much to charge for my services. I figured, well, this guy's been doing this for fifteen years and I'm just starting. So he should make at least twice as much as I do. But he insisted, no, we're both psychiatrists, we should both charge the same. I thought, you've got to be kidding. I don't even know what I'm doing."

With his years of training, Ken was probably more competent than he realized, but it still took five years of "practice and experience and some successes and some ability to tolerate lack of success" before he *felt* competent. "I can finally relax now," he observes. "It's kind of like riding a horse or driving a car. I don't have to clutch the steering wheel so tight anymore."

Unlike Ken Phillips, graphic designer Tim Botts thought he was competent long before he really was. "I wasn't very good when I first got out of art school," he says, "but I thought I was. I thought I was wonderful. But looking back on my earliest designs, I can see that some of them were just really bad—even though they were always creative and different—because I was just learning and experimenting. Fortunately, the company I was working with didn't know enough back then to know when my designs weren't very good. So I had a lot of freedom to explore."

Tim credits that freedom, along with a good art education and years of rubbing shoulders with other designers at professional association meetings, with helping to mature his natural talents into genuine competence.

While most people who love their work say they feel competent in the doing of their work, many say they are also acutely aware that competence is not a plateau to be reached once and for all, but a mountain with no summit. You must always be climbing higher.

College president David Horner is a good example of the many work lovers whose strong sense of basic competence is accompanied by extremely high standards—which keep them striving. Every year, David goes through an evaluation process with the board of his college. He evaluates his own performance and then compares his conclusions with those of board members. "So far," says David, "my evaluations of myself have been lower than their evaluations of me. I give myself about a three on a five-point scale. But I still have a sense of competence because I see the job as very, very difficult. So my self-evaluation doesn't reflect a sense that I'm not competent, but my judgment of the difficulty of the task."

Unlike some work lovers, David feels less competent now than he did when he first accepted a college presidency at the unheard-of age of twenty-nine. "I'd probably rate myself lower now than I would have when I was thirty years old," he observes, "not because I'm doing a poorer job or I'm less skilled—I've learned every year and have probably gotten better at my job every year—but my sense of what could be done keeps going out farther.

"But just as I don't think I could love my work if I didn't think I was good at it, I don't think I could continue to love my work if it lost that stretching component."

Ron Nikkel, president of Prison Fellowship International, echoes the sense of duality that many work lovers say they feel. "I have a basic sense of competence," he says, "but I feel the same way about my work as I do about climbing a mountain. I wouldn't tackle it if I didn't think I have the basic experience and capability to cope with it, but there's always this fear that this might be the one that does me in.

"I have confidence in my capabilities, but I also have a sense of inadequacy in the face of the task," he continues. "There is so much that can be done and I can only do an infinitesimal piece of it. The task is overwhelming. The mountain is overwhelming. But I have the competence to take a step at a time."

Understanding the importance of moving step by step up the mountain seems to be critical to achieving competence—and loving your work. The side effect is two-way vision: you can always look down and see how far you've come, but you can always look up and see how far you have to go. Marlene LeFever: "Yes, I feel competent. Yes, I feel totally incompetent. The two feelings fight each other and I'm not sure that's bad.

"I'm forty-seven years old," she says, "and I certainly have not achieved everything I want to, but I've done enough that I can look at my little pile and say, 'Oh, well, look at that, I've done that.' I can say, 'In the past, I've achieved.' It's taken a lot of education. I'm leaving soon for a course I'm taking with the Association for Curriculum Supervision and Development. That's my field, but I'll be there like any other student. That teacher has something to teach me that I don't know a thing about. And I need to. So being competent involves the ability to say, 'Hey, I'm dumb here but I'm going to get smarter.' "

Photographer Jim Steere discovered that one of the benefits of "getting smarter" about your work—of increasing your competence—is increased knowledge of what you're good at and really love doing. Jim says he's amazed at how his skill level has improved in the five years since he first launched a professional career in photography and at how that has increased his ability to enjoy his work. "I've gotten to a place in the last couple of years where I can see a consistency in what I produce," he says. "There's a consistent level of quality that makes me feel that I really am a professional. Somewhere along the line, you have to cross that threshold. You have to get to a place where you feel competent, where you can say, 'Sure, I can do that.' And when you get to that point, you also develop the confidence to say sometimes, 'No, that's not really what I either want to do or am capable of doing.'

"When I first started, I would do almost anything anybody wanted me to do—no matter how boring or dumb or over my head it was. Now I'm at a point where I'm more willing to turn down work and say, 'I really just don't want to do that anymore' or 'That's not what I'm good at.' "

A sense of basic competence seems to be critical to loving your work. But competence isn't something you're born with—it requires time and training and experience. What's more, it is not necessarily a status you achieve once and for all—it's more like a continuum with no end. People who love their work the most seem to combine a strong sense of basic competence with an equally strong sense of continuing challenge in their work. Work lovers are stretched but not unduly stressed. They know they are good at what they do, but they strive to be better. Like Ron Nikkel, they say, "The mountain is overwhelming. But I have the competence to take one step at a time."

8

The People Factor: Working in Community

———

"MY MOTHER TOLD ME ONCE THAT WHEN I WAS A LITTLE GIRL, I USED to stand on the porch and call out 'Come and play with me,' to the people walking by," says Alice Rubash, smiling at the recollection. "There's something about me that's still like that. I'm still saying to people, 'Come and play with me.' "

Alice is the volunteer director of her congregation's Stephen Ministry, a program which links volunteer caregivers with parishioners who need emotional and practical support. An attractive woman in her late fifties who exudes warmth and humor, Alice has a master's degree in social work but has chosen to use her skills without pay in a multitude of volunteer positions in cities throughout the world. As the wife of an oil executive, she has moved back and forth between countries and continents so often that she no longer thinks of any one place as home. But everywhere she goes, she finds a way to exercise her three-pronged vocation—caregiving, teaching and building community.

Building community is both a part of her work and a prerequisite for doing it, Alice says. "I must do my work in community," she emphasizes. "I couldn't do it alone. When we were building the Stephen Ministry team, for example, there was a lot of 'Let's have breakfast together.' And I'm not afraid to be the person who calls and says, 'Let's have breakfast.' It's as if I'm still saying to people, 'Come and play with me.'

"I like to be part of a group," she continues, "and I like to help other people become part of a group. I'm good at it, I enjoy it and I think it's important."

Alice Rubash isn't famous, but she has something in common with someone who is—well-known church historian Martin Marty. They both understand the importance of being part of a group, of working in community.

"It could be that somewhere there's a Tolstoyan hermit who's changing the world in a great way," says the white-haired scholar, "but for the long pull, I believe meaning and reward in work happens in community. At an annual faculty lecture, one of our great astrophysicists said that in the 1940s, fellow faculty members chipped in their gas rationing stamps so he could make a ninety-mile trip twice a week to an observatory with two students. But, he said, it was cost effective because two years later he won a Nobel Prize and ten years later the students did. There was a symbiosis there. He grew while they grew. So I think it's important to find or invent community.

"The person who is responsible only to himself or herself probably takes too much pride in their own achievement and is shattered when something goes wrong. The letter of rejection from a publisher—oh, that hurts. But a letter of rejection that comes on a day when a lot of other things are happening, because I'm surrounded by community, is not as difficult.

"If you get a scratch in a piece of sterling and take it to a silversmith to buff it," he continues, picking up two spoons to demonstrate, "he'll say, 'Oh, that's designed for thousands of tooth marks and thousands of scratches. Eventually, it will acquire a patina that's more beautiful than when it was new.' It's the same way with interactions at work. After daily repetitions of this (he scratches the two spoons together), you get a patina."

Patina or no, most people, I've discovered, find it a lot easier to enjoy their work when it's done in community. Consequently, work lovers are, for the most part, people who have been able to find community:

□ Rich Berg, bond salesman: I'm dependent on a lot of people to do my work. I work with a trader, an underwriter, a partner and another trader. It makes the work-flow far superior and is very important. I wouldn't want to do my work alone. If my company offered to let me set up an office at home, I wouldn't do it.

□ Kurt Neradt, dry wall taper: I like working and associating with blue-collar workers. The white-collar workers I used to work with never seemed to want to take time to say hi, and when they did, it never seemed to be sincere. It's not that way with the guys I work with now. Plus, I usually work with a good friend of mine, Mike, and that helps a lot too.

□ Peter Baker, pediatrician: A small doctor's office is like a family. You have to have bonds of mutual respect going to sustain any kind of long-term relationship. And I like that.

□ Telva Urban, dialysis nurse: Community is what I like most about what I do. The average dialysis patient comes in to the hospital three times a week for three to four hours at a time so I get to develop a rapport with them and their families over a period of time. A lot of my patients I've known for eight years— ever since I started working at this hospital.

□ Elizabeth Cody Newenhuyse, author/journalist: There's something about being part of a really good creative team, which is what we have on our magazine staff. We get along well. We tend to think alike about a lot of things. We have the same quirky humor. We have weekly prayer as a staff. We share a lot of things. To be part of a group of literate, thinking, fun Christians is for me like a dream come true. It feels like I have a second family.

☐ David Horner, college president: I enjoy the people I work with. We laugh a lot. We go out and eat a lot. And we also worship together. If I'm feeling some pain about something, I can talk to people here about it. It's crucial to me not only that I'm interested in and enjoy my work, but that I'm interested in and enjoy the people I'm working with.

Businessman/entrepreneur Gary Ginter says that community is one of the characteristics of not only enjoyable work, but what he calls "authentic work." "I suppose it's possible to have an authentic call to solo work," he muses, "but I can't imagine it's healthy. Even the artist needs to be in community. We are social beings. God has called us to be together. And since we spend more time at work than in our families, work is where community happens."

People who are successful in work are much more likely to be happy in their work than those who aren't, but Gary discounts the idea that superachievers are Lone Ranger superstars. "The press is always looking for the superhero, the insightful, incredible visionary, the ball of fire who stands tall above her fellowmen," he says. "But such people are pretty rare. More commonly, the successful entrepreneur is all of those things, but with a generous sprinkling of weaknesses that are all too evident in the heat of battle. I think that if you look at the great entrepreneurs in the United States, if you study them carefully, you'd find they're not the sole reason for the success of their businesses. There's always a team behind them."

That's great for people who *have* a team. But what about artists and writers and doctors who are solo practitioners—and people in scores of other solitary professions? They have no built-in community. Is it possible to love their work despite its absence? Or can they find a way to create it?

Writer and publishing executive Marlene LeFever says the writing aspect of her work is *not* done in community and she loves it anyway. "When I write an article and I'm interrupted by someone, it's like bringing me back from somewhere I want to be and forcing me to do something I don't want to do," she says. "I'm not sure there is such a thing as a community creation."

Creative artist Dick Winzeler disagrees. He says he's worked alone and worked in community—and community is better. "When I started writing, I did it by myself," he recalls, "and then I realized that we all have certain gifts and that maybe I could take advantage of that and blend mine with someone else's. So I started writing with other people. Now I think that community and support and feedback from fellow musicians and writers and actors is really important. I know now that I need a supportive structure. I believe that creative people especially need community."

Upon further reflection, Marlene LeFever relents a bit. "I have people around me who support me when I need the support, and the spirit among us when we're working on a project together is communal," she admits. "So I know the difference that community support can make."

I found it interesting that, with a few exceptions, work lovers told me that community was a critically important variable in their ability to love their work. And yet, a striking number of work lovers interviewed for this book work alone, or in positions that by their nature isolate them. So for these people, community is something they've had to find—or create.

Consider these work lovers who have found a way to circumvent an inherent lack of community in their work:

☐ Jack Stockman, illustrator: Lack of community has been one of my biggest problems as a free-lancer. A big, big problem. Even my most regular customers I only relate to about three times a year. So it's difficult to get any substantive relationship going. One partial solution has been to meet with three other guys for breakfast, which I've been doing for the last ten years.

☐ Kevin Miller, magazine editor: One of the biggest adjustments for me in my current job has been doing most of my work alone. One of the things I loved about my last job was the fact that I really felt like part of a team, which was fun. So I compensate by occasionally dropping in on my former colleagues and shooting the breeze with them. I also meet once a week with a friend who works for the same organization. He tells me what's going on in his life, and I tell him what's going on in mine and we pray for each other. We've done that for about a year and a half and it's been really great. It's really given me a sense of community.

☐ Ann Anderson, mother: It's true in some ways that you're isolated as an at-home mother. You can go several days without hearing another adult voice for most of the day. You do your work alone, or at least you're not working with any other adults. But I think there are lots of ways not to be isolated. I get together with other friends who have children, meet them at the park, go to the zoo. I've also found that getting involved in my sons' preschool is a good way to meet other moms. And I hire a baby sitter every Thursday so I have a day off. That is very important to me.

☐ Ken Phillips, psychiatrist: One of the main reasons I started this practice, besides the financial stuff, is the fact that it provides a community. I've tried to model it after a group of Christian psychiatrists, psychologists and social workers I worked with during my residency. People with similar values were working together in the same space, sharing cases, supporting each other and having fun together. There was a sense of community there. I've done both—I've worked in a little cubicle, and I've worked in a group practice. This is much better because of the community.

☐ Tim Botts, graphic designer: I enjoy working with other people and find it stimulating to rub shoulders and interact with them. But for many years, the people who worked for me were not as talented as I am and I wasn't challenged by them. There were some exceptions along the way and even more so now—some of the people I work with now really challenge me and that's good. But it wasn't always that way. So I belong to three different professional organizations that have really stretched me. I go to an international calligraphy convention each year, for example, and rub shoulders with the best calligraphers in the world. I take classes from them, teach alongside them—and then come back each year recharged with new ideas. It's very, very important.

☐ Karen Mains, author: I create community. I take my tin cup and go begging for it. I've just come through a period of exceeding loneliness and I've realized that I can't function solo. So I went to Word Publishing and they gave me a grant of $10,000 to pull a writers' group together. We have twenty-one of us who meet yearly and we do projects to sustain ourselves. I need that.

It's become a cliché to point out how easy it is to feel lonely in the middle of a crowd. But people who have to create their own community because they work alone may not immediately understand how elusive a commodity it can be for others—even for people who work in a large group. One of the most difficult places to find community can be at the top of an organization, as Greg Darnieder, executive director of a growing social service agency, has discovered.

"When we were smaller, we had a greater sense of community," he observes. "It was easier to do things together as an entire staff.

But as we've gotten larger and developed a layer of middle management, other people are handling some of the day-to-day things I'm used to doing. And that removes me from some of the more intimate interactions. In giving that up, I've had to redefine some of the relationships I've had with people over a period of thirteen years. There's a separation, a loneliness, about that that I don't like."

Greg loves his work despite the increasing degree of isolation he feels, but he's working on ways to regain some of the sense of community he felt in years past. If he's successful, he believes he'll be able to enjoy his work even more.

Greg might be interested in the experience of Ken Smith, who, as the CEO of a successful mid-size corporation, is a prime candidate for the proverbial loneliness that so many people seem to feel at the top. But he believes in the importance of community and has found ways to create it for himself and his employees.

"I don't think God has called any of us to be lone rangers," he says. "We need the support and encouragement of fellow believers, no matter who we are or where we are. I have that here in this company. My fellow directors are men I can pray with. We have quite a number of believers in this company. I've never insisted that my employees have the same spiritual convictions that I do— we try to hire the best people we can get for a particular job given they have ethical standards and values—but believers seem to gravitate here. And I have led a Bible study for over twenty years that is open to anybody in the company. So I have contact with people all down the line who love the Lord."

Despite the ideal of the church as an ultimate example of Christian community, pastors are particularly vulnerable to loneliness and isolation in their work. Genuine community requires a level of openness, vulnerability and transparency that pastors often feel they can't exhibit as the spiritual leader of a congregation. Whether their feelings are self-imposed or externally imposed, ministers often believe that they must maintain an appearance of spiritual and emotional invincibility. This may gain them respect, but it rarely allows them to enjoy a sense of community.

Dean Leuking is an exception to the stereotype of the isolated congregational shepherd. He says the sense of community he finds in his vocation is one of the prime reasons he has loved his role as pastor of a large midwestern church for over thirty-six years.

"The people of this place and the colleagues on my staff are no small reason I love the work," he explains. "I am a partner with other people, not a lord over them or an answer man to every person. My colleagues and I are a team—I can give my gifts and they give theirs. We forgive each other when we step on each others' toes. And that happens. We don't live in a make-believe world. We're not perfect. I have to be honest about my failings and faults with my colleagues, as they are about theirs. So when we hit snags in our day-to-day work, it doesn't deliver an earthquake shock to the whole enterprise. We can back off of it, cool down and talk to each other. We listen to each other. We respect and learn from each other. The outcome is a better vocational sense that I work with people I'm here to serve.

"I've learned that I have to let my faults show. When I have egg on my face, I try not to say, 'I'm the pastor. I can't have egg on my face.' Community means being human, being honest, being candid about the fact that I'm not perfect. I have moments when I'm short of temper and I can show that. But when I lose my cool and say things I wish I had shut my mouth about, I can say to people, 'Please forgive me.' That's what creates community.

"Forgiveness of sins is the way that the twenty-four people here on our staff demonstrate to each other that we're part of a community. It takes the pressure off of turf protection, games playing, manipulation and holding back from frustration and anger. When we care enough about each other to take each other seriously, to affirm each other's gifts and to ask hard questions of each other, it creates a genuineness about community instead of a somewhat fanciful, contrived and rather shallow appearance of community." Having worked to create a sense of community in his daily work, Dean has found that he also needs another level of community on a periodic basis. "I have a confessor," he says, "someone I can go to freely and talk to about things I've said or done. I think that's essential to community. I don't go to anybody and everybody about the things that are deeply troubling to my spirit, things that wound my conscience. I go to a person who is well equipped for that and outside my immediate circle."

It's interesting to me that even people who don't have a community around them in the doing of their work seem to be able to enjoy their work more if they experience community somewhere in their lives. Community outside of work is what we usually refer to as friendship. Martin Marty: "What plays a big part in any form of work is the constancy of friendship. I think that in terms of getting strokes and admonition, friends are as important as anyone in the workplace. A friend is someone who comes along and says, 'This time you've gone too far.' And it's not as threatening as if the boss has to call you down. You can tell the difference between people who have friends and people who don't. President Nixon had no friends. Jim Bakker and Jimmy Swaggart had no friends. Billy Graham has friends. It's important."

Work lovers differ in how much community they require—and what they think it is—but with very few exceptions they seem to have incorporated it into their lives and found a way to make it support their vocation. Like Karen Mains, they get out their tin cup and go begging for it. Like Kevin Miller, they saunter down the hall in search of it. Like Alice Rubash, they aren't afraid to call out, "Come and play with me. Let's do this together."

9

Earning Enough Money

"For the love of money is a root of all kinds of evil. . . ."
1 TIMOTHY 6:10

"Financial reward is probably more important than any of us realize."
**KEN SMITH,
CORPORATE CEO**

"No man but a blockhead ever wrote except for money."
**SAMUEL JOHNSON
BOSWELL'S LIFE OF JOHNSON**

JUDY EVERSWICK, A VOCATIONAL COUNSELOR AT A LARGE MIDWESTERN high school, says many of her young counselees make more working part-time at McDonalds than she does working thirty-five to forty hours a week at the school. And yet she passionately loves her work.

Judy Everswick is an exception.

When I first started interviewing for this book, I made a casual assumption that money would not be an important variable in loving one's work. After all, I thought, if you're truly passionate about your work, compensation is a minor issue. I was wrong. Wrong, wrong, wrong.

The overwhelming consensus of work lovers I talked to was this: Money struggles are likely to take the joy out of your work, even work that you would otherwise love.

Judy Everswick, of course, stands as an exception to that rule. A former missionary to Africa, Judy came back to the States when her husband took an administrative job with their mission. But she discovered that she was a "fish out of water" as an American housewife. So she jumped at the chance to work at the local high school, counseling kids about colleges and vocations. "I loved it from the first day I got in there," she says. "I love the kids. I'm not there to give them grades, to be a parent to them, to keep the car from them or ground them. So the kids feel free to open up and share. And I love being available to them."

The kids love her, as was evident when they excitedly presented her with a huge bouquet of roses following the most recent all-school variety show. "Thanks for caring about us," a hulking football player said with an affectionate hug.

"With things like that happening to me," says Judy, "I'd work a million hours even if they paid me nothing."

It almost came to that. A couple of years ago, school officials told her that the grant money which funded her position had been used up. "I'll do it for nothing," she told them. "God has given me so many opportunities with the kids and the faculty that I can't imagine doing anything else." The school found some money to pay her, but Judy still makes a fraction of what she could earn in almost any other job.

Despite her genuine love of her work, even Judy admits that she's occasionally been tempted to look for a position that would allow her to pay a bigger percentage of the family bills.

"Making a lot of money isn't important for my self-worth," she says, "but sometimes I do get this panicky feeling. My husband is a missionary getting paid a missionary salary. We just put two kids in college and one of the kids needs braces. Somebody saying, 'I can't believe the change in the attitude of the student council since you've been working with them' gives me all the satisfaction I need in my work. But I do start feeling frustrated when I ask myself, Should I be doing more for our family financially?"

That same question plagues Jack Stockman. Jack is an extraordinarily talented and, in his words, "moderately well known" freelance illustrator who nonetheless struggles on a regular basis with the financial exigencies of his business. Jack can make a very respectable income in the course of a year and still not be able to pay his bills on a consistent basis because of cash flow problems. "I might have $20,000 worth of outstanding billings at any given time that I can't bill until I finish an entire project," Jack explains. "And even after I bill a client, it may be sixty to ninety days before I get paid. So that's why my wife and I had to borrow money from a friend to pay the rent this month. We hated doing it, but we had no choice."

Jack loves illustration. He's good at it. He believes that God made him an artist for a purpose. And yet, money problems are siphoning away some of the joy in his work.

"If I didn't have to worry about money I'd be a lot more satisfied," he admits. "The money thing totally dominates my life. And talking with other artists, they say it totally dominates their lives.

"Sometimes I get really angry at God. I'll tell him, 'Why did you make me this way? Why did you put me in this situation where I don't have rent money this month?' My only recourse is to remember that he promises to give me peace, to never leave me or forsake me. And then I'll say, 'So what does it mean for you not to leave me if you don't supply money for food this month?' "

If you ask Jack if he loves his work, he'll say yes. But it's a qualified yes. He'd love it a lot more if he didn't have to worry about money. So much for the stereotype of the starving artist blissfully toiling away in a freezing garret, so focused on his work that he is unaware of hunger, cold and poverty.

Actually, it's not all that hard to believe that, with rare exceptions, people who are struggling to survive find it difficult to love their work. But what about people whose survival needs are met? Is money a variable in their ability to love their work?

Absolutely. Because, like it or not, "good pay" communicates worth. Consider the comments of just a few of the many work lovers I talked to who testified to the relationship between their compensation and their work satisfaction:

☐ Marlene LeFever, writer and publishing executive: I don't go home with bags of money, but I'm paid fairly. I think it's important. Money is an indication to many people, myself included, that I am of worth. I wish I could take my total "worthhood" from what I do and from internal sources. But I can't. So when I get a raise or when I get money for what I do, it's an affirmation of what other people think of me.

☐ Kerry Berg, mother: It took me awhile to adjust to not making money after my daughter was born. Before I quit working I was a sales assistant to the branch manager of a brokerage house, and whenever I did anything well my boss would reward me not only verbally but financially. So it was a tough adjustment to stay home. Sometimes I'll tell my husband, "I need your approval sometimes because I'm not making money."

☐ Ken Smith, CEO, financial services firm: I can't remember a time, especially since I've become a Christian, that I was consumed with making a whole lot of money. But in the marketplace, financial reward is probably more important than any of us realize. I don't think I'd have liked what I was doing all these years nearly as much if the financial rewards hadn't been there. That's how everything is measured.

☐ Karen Mains, writer: We try to live simply and trust the Lord to provide for our needs. He always has, but we've never had excess. Having lived that way so long, I feel like making a lot of money isn't a motivating consideration. But I feel good about being able to contribute significantly. I don't make big amounts of dollars, but I make about half of our family income. And that gives me a great sense of independence and autonomy. I also think that my husband respects what I do because I'm a wage earner. You can't get around it.

Based on comments like these, it would seem that the key to loving one's work is to find a job that will pay you as much as possible. But it's important to note that most of the work lovers I interviewed are *not* primarily motivated by money. They are, for the most part, people who pursued their gifts and interests and found a way to be well compensated—or feel well compensated—for doing the work that they loved.

Of course, the definition of what it means to be well compensated differs from person to person. Every year we read stories in the sports pages about professional athletes who are holding out for more money, even though they're already making what would seem to be a fortune by other people's standards. I find it hard to imagine being dissatisfied with an income of, say, $500,000 a year. But if you're comparing yourself to somebody else in your profession who's making $1 million a year—somebody who is no more talented or diligent or effective than you are—it's hard to love your work. Or so it seems.

On the other hand, if you're comparing your income to that of someone who's living below the poverty line, you can feel well paid enough to love your work even if your salary is very modest. Take Greg Darnieder, for example.

Greg, who directs an inner-city social service program, has never made much money. He and his family live in a Chicago neighborhood that many suburbanites would be afraid to walk in after dark.

For years, it was a bittersweet joke in the family that they couldn't take vacations because the family car was too unreliable to take on a long trip. Finances were, and are, tight. Despite that fact, over the years Greg tried to turn down many of the raises his board insisted on giving him. When the members of the board threatened to resign if he didn't accept an increase, he finally agreed to take it. But somehow the extra money never made it to his paycheck.

"I told my wife I was taking the increase," he admits ruefully. "I told my board I was. But for the sake of maybe increasing somebody else's salary or buying something we needed for the program, I didn't actually take it. I felt guilty making what I felt was more than enough money working in a neighborhood where the average family income is incredibly small."

With the strong encouragement of his wife and his board, Greg is now accepting the small raises his budget allows. Still, by the standards of many middle-class Americans, Greg Darnieder's salary is very modest. But by the standards of the poor people Greg works with —people whose average income falls far below what the U.S. government calls the poverty line—Greg is extraordinarily well paid.

Greg chooses to take the latter view, which is one of many reasons he loves his work.

Although financial compensation appears to be an important variable in loving one's work, it seems to be a poor reason for choosing a vocation. Just ask Kurt Neradt. Kurt had always dreamed of getting a job selling bonds like his friend Brad. Brad made a lot of money—enough to buy a big new house, a Jaguar and a Rolex watch. So when Kurt had an opportunity to leave his job as a food salesman and get into selling bonds, he jumped at the chance— even though he had never really enjoyed sales. "I figured I was going to go where the pie in the sky was," observes Kurt. "I wanted to make a lot of money whether I enjoyed the work or not."

So for a year and a half, Kurt struggled to succeed in the bond business. "I put my heart and soul into it," he recalls. "I really worked hard, but I just couldn't make it. It got to the point where I would go to bed on Sunday night and think, 'Oh, no, I've got to go to work tomorrow.' "

Kurt didn't make it in the bond business—even though he was extremely motivated to make money—because he was ignoring his true gifts and interests. When he finally started thinking about the activities he truly enjoyed—working with his hands, taking something that looks like a disaster and making it look good—he found the line of work that he now loves: dry wall taping. Interestingly, Kurt says that the financial security he has found in his new profession is an important element in his love of his work. But he had to find work that he could enjoy, work he was gifted to do, before he could find financial security. He doesn't have a Jaguar or a Rolex watch, but it no longer matters. "Money is important," he says. "I wouldn't do what I'm doing for nothing. But after what my wife and I went through when I was selling bonds, now it seems like I'm making double."

Rich Blackburn spent several years pursuing his dream of being "the relative with the second and third vacation home to which I would invite everybody." Rich accepted it as something of a given that making a lot of money should be his goal. "I knew exactly what I'd do with the money," he says today, "everything from buying Jaguars to touring castles in my spare time."

Although he was very successful as a salesman, Rich found he couldn't tolerate the tedium of the typical business workday. So he became a teacher, a profession he loves despite the relatively modest pay. Now he feels sorry for people who seem trapped in their quest for "big bucks."

"I can't tell you how many people have said to me, 'I wish I could do what you're doing. But I couldn't function at even the highest salary level in the education field.' They tell me to my face that they're miserable, that they don't like getting up in the morning. I have a friend, for example, who sells widgits for a very successful firm in New York City. Every time I see him he talks about how much he hates the Madison Avenue scene, how much he wants to get out. Why is it that so many people I know feel like they're on a treadmill and can't get off?"

Woodworker David Orth has an answer: "If your primary goal is to make money, your joy is going to suffer." David should know. It took him years to seriously consider woodworking as a vocation because he never saw it as a way to make a living. Once he allowed himself to pursue the work that he loved, he found that he could make a living—a modest living, but a living. Enough of a living to enable him to continue loving his work.

Not everyone is as fortunate as David Orth. Some people pursue the vocation they love and find that financial struggles have taken the joy out of it. Some people pursue the vocation they love and find they can't support themselves and their family. Some people support themselves doing the work they love but, because of whom they're comparing themselves to, are unable to feel well paid—and consequently are unable to sustain the joy in their work.

But some people, those who seem to love their work the most, experience the delight of being well paid, or feeling well paid, for doing the work that gives them joy.

Pediatrician Peter Baker is one such person. "I was lucky enough to stumble onto a niche that I like a lot and that pays pretty well," he says. "Even though pediatricians tend to fall toward the lower end of the income level of physicians, we're doing okay and that's nice. Newspaper columnist Sidney Harris said once that one of the joys of his life was to be paid well for something he enjoyed doing and maybe would do even if he weren't paid so well. That's how I feel. To be paid well for something I really enjoy doing is very satisfying."

Work lovers have a lot to say about money, and their comments are worth hearing:

☐ David Himelick, carpenter/building contractor: I would start out by asking myself, "What would I do if I didn't have to worry about money?" You have to factor it in eventually, but I think a lot of people worry too much about the end product of money and forget to make sure they love their job. I think it's real important to start with what you love because it seems like a lot of people who are doing what they love are making money too.

☐ Marlene LeFever, publishing executive/writer: Money is an important variable in loving your work. I don't think I would be happy if I had to struggle, if I had to think for three weeks about whether or not I could go out to dinner one night, if I had to drive a car that was held together with safety pins.

☐ Greg Darnieder, director, inner-city tutoring ministry: I've just recently started getting in touch with my responsibility to my family when it comes to money. It's one thing to be self-sacrificing myself, but when it's taking away from my family, that raises some serious issues that I haven't always been in touch with.

☐ Jim Steere, free-lance photographer: I started out in the photography business with the idealistic idea that it's more important to do what you really love than to make money, but now that I have kids and several years of free-lance photography behind me, some of the shine has worn off. At some point you realize that you have responsibilities besides just satisfying your own interests. Money becomes more important. If your love for what you're doing isn't rewarded in a way that makes the rest of your life easier to manage, it can really kill the love you have for what you're doing. If I were single, having a meager existence would probably be okay, but when there are other people you're responsible for, it's not okay. In fact, it's probably pretty selfish. So money has become much more important than I thought it would be.

☐ Elizabeth Cody Newenhuyse, author/journalist: Money has a lot to do with my love of my work. If nobody was paying me to write, I'd probably still do it, but I wouldn't devote as much time to it. To have pride in your work is important and pride comes not only from knowing you've done a good job, but from other people recognizing it too. Since we don't live in Utopia, people who do good jobs get rewarded monetarily.

☐ Robert Gross, chiropractor: I have a passion for my work, but right now, all the pressure with money is watering down that passion. I keep saying to myself, "God will provide. Just go and serve people." I don't want to become money-oriented. But it's so difficult because the bills are flying in and the money isn't. I was making a lot of money in the family business, but I hated it. I couldn't get up in the morning and face the place. Now I love my work, but there's a lot of apprehension because of the money.

☐ Chuck Swirsky, sportscaster: I have to be honest. Being paid well contributes to my enjoyment of my work.

☐ Harold Myra, publishing executive: Young people all seem to be saying, "What's it going to pay?" It never even entered my mind to think about what something is going to pay, only if I would really be able to focus in on the job and enjoy it. Money is a factor, but it isn't as important as the intensity with which one can approach one's work. I wasn't looking for money. Adequate money came, but strictly as a by-product of the intensity and the love of the work. If you're doing something that gives you great enjoyment and there's enough money to survive in reasonable shape, I'd say you should probably stay with it.

☐ Sandy Rios, singer: I don't think I could ever do something just for the money. But when I'm really busy and working hard and making good money, it gives me a lot of pride. I feel really satisfied that I can contribute to my family.

☐ John Folkening, church music director: When I was a kid and told people I wanted to be a Lutheran school teacher and church music director when I grew up, they said, "But there's no money in that." I had all the right answers. I told them, "The Lord will provide." And to a certain extent, the Lord has provided. We've been able to buy a house, for example. But if I were to get a call about another job, the first thing I'd ask is, "What's the salary? If I can't afford it, why are we even talking about it?" I've gotten a lot more practical as I've gotten older. I'm not just accountable for me—I've got five people in my family. If I can't make things work financially, I wouldn't be worth a shot of powder anyway.

☐ Gary Ginter, businessman: I wouldn't want to do work that didn't make money, because profits matter: they show you're doing something worthwhile. But I don't care if I make a lot or a little. The money isn't why you're doing it. You're doing it because you should do it, because it's right and because being a Christian means finding a match between how God has put you together—your gifts and abilities—and the requirements of your job.

Making a lot of money is a bad reason, if it's the only reason, for choosing a vocation. In fact, your chances of succeeding at making large sums of money in a profession are greatly reduced if you don't inherently love the work. But make no mistake, it is very difficult—almost impossible—to love your work if you can't support yourself and your family, if you're constantly struggling to make ends meet or if you have a chronic sense of being underpaid.

If, however, you can find a way to be well paid, or feel well paid, in the process of exercising your gifts and pursuing your passions, you have a very good chance of loving your work.

10

Expressing Your Faith Through Your Work

"My work makes my faith more meaningful and my faith makes my work more meaningful."
DAVID ORTH,
WOODWORKER

MOST OF THE WORK LOVERS I INTERVIEWED FOR THIS BOOK ARE PEO-
ple of strong faith. They love God and want to please him. They
go about their lives with a spiritual consciousness. They listen for
God's voice and try to act on what they hear. They seek to live out
their faith-based values in the multitude of moments that make up
daily existence. Knowing this, I wasn't surprised that it is important
to them—and by extrapolation to most people of faith who love
their work—that their daily labors be an expression of their relationship to God.

How that happens differs by the individual. For some, faith is the
motivation for their work. For others, faith has more to do with the
content or quality or manner of their work. Still others see their
work as an act of obedience to God, an act of creativity in imitation
of God, or an act of service to God. Some work lovers speak of their

faith as a support undergirding their work or as the overarching force guiding the totality of their lives, out of which work cannot be separated. Different people with different experiences, but one commonality: their faith is part of their work, and their work is part of their faith.

Faith as a Motivation for Work

When high-school English teacher Richard Blackburn is asked how his spiritual values interact with his work, he responds by referring to one of his favorite movies, *Indiana Jones and the Last Crusade.* "Remember when Indy comes in and interrupts his father just as he's recording an inscription from a medieval medallion?" he asks a visitor to his classroom. "The inscription says, 'May he who illuminated this illuminate you.'

"Ever since I saw that film, I've been thinking about illumination, about divinity intervening in human history. Of Christ coming as a teacher, as a great storyteller who used metaphor to convey truth.

"I believe in objective truth in the universe," the burly teacher says, leaning forward in his intensity. "I believe in the Promethean torch, in guiding someone closer to an objective truth which may ultimately lead them to a spiritual experience.

"When I teach someone how to write a sentence instead of a fragment," he continues, "they're a little closer to understanding the form and design and intelligence of the universe. When I teach literature, I'm helping my students find objective truth. The truth in *Macbeth* is that ambition unchecked leads to disaster. Hamlet stops himself from committing suicide because he's afraid he'll jeopardize the life to come—a very Christian concept. The last scene in *King Lear* is basically a scene of forgiveness and recon-ciliation.

"The motivation for my work is illumination—guiding someone closer to the light of the universe."

Faith as the Content of Work

Some work lovers say that one reason they are able to love their work is the fact that they can express their faith through the *content* of their work.

One such work lover is graphic designer Tim Botts. "As an artist, I work from content," he says. "I derive my inspiration from creation, from what I see around me. Everything I work from is already here. I design after the Creator. Since there's a tendency toward a lot of irrationality in much of today's art, I try to imitate the orderliness of creation. I try to be rational in my thought processes, even though there is a beauty to randomness. If you throw a bunch of things up in the air and watch them fall down there can be a wonderful spontaneity in the resulting design. But within randomness there is order."

Then there are those, like Martin Marty, who deal with the stuff of faith on a daily basis. "My faith is storied," he says, "and I get paid to tell stories. Historians are record keepers who make the past present. I believe the Holy Spirit takes old stories and makes the past present. I think the Holy Spirit is the one who keeps us from being a burial society or keeping a city of the dead. The gospel is now. Fresh.

"I've written about the church in Russia and about pacifists in World War 2. They're all part of the unfolding story. None of them prove the existence of God and about none of them can I say, 'This is exactly what God had in mind.' But I have a feeling that I'm involved in something that's very important.

"I think the Christian faith impels us to keep the theme of suffering before us. I don't think you'd need a doctrine of God if there weren't suffering, and I don't think there would be a problem of God if there weren't suffering. I don't think you'd have good history or good poetry if you don't deal with it. I don't think you have good ministry if you evade it.

"Theodor Adorno has said that most of the human story is suffering and not to tell that story is to dishonor the sufferers. I think that's especially true in the context of the Christian faith. Not ever to tell the story of the Baptists in Russia who endured for seventy-two years is to dishonor their faith. To tell the story is to build upon the fruit of their faith. They won't always be happy stories. But they will be stories of the working out of faith. So I attempt to contribute to the faith by telling stories."

Faith and the Manner of Work

When asked about the connection between their work and their faith, many work lovers talked about the manner in which they do their work. Some frequent themes: Honesty, quality, concern for others.

Expressing Faith through Honesty

Honesty, work lovers agree, is an expression of faith at its most basic level. There is a fundamental satisfaction in doing one's work with integrity even when it hurts.

"My faith costs me money at times," admits bond salesman Rich Berg. "Although some of the securities I sell are very black and white—I can define your risk absolutely and I can tell you what your return is going to be—some other securities I can jiggle a little bit. I can tell you your yield and the guy down the street can sell the same security and make it sound a lot better. I could do that but I would be bending my ethics. I will never intentionally hurt anybody. I will not bend my Christian standards for the sake of a dollar. I would have a hard time enjoying my work if I had to intentionally cheat somebody."

For dialysis nurse Telva Urban, the satisfaction that honesty brings comes at a cost of, not money, but convenience. "It's so easy to lie to patients about their treatment so they won't give us a hard time," she says. "One of the things dialysis does is remove water from the blood of patients. But if the water comes out too fast, the patient can get sick. So we have a knob on the dialysis machine that's called 'negative pressure.' A lot of patients quibble with us because they don't want their negative pressure set as high as we think it should be. So some of the nurses just set it where they think it should be and never tell the patient. But I always sit down with the patient and say, 'Here's the deal. If the pressure is too high, you'll get sick. So this is why I think we should do this.' To me, it's just not right to not inform a patient about what's going on with their treatment."

Expressing Faith through Quality

Magazine editor Kevin Miller is exemplary of those who say they express their faith through the quality of their work. "I'm not sure it's a strictly Christian virtue," he says, "but I have a real commitment to excellence. I'm a fanatic about accuracy. I want readers to be able to really trust my magazine. I want them to open any page or look at any photo caption and say, 'I know I can trust this information.' To me, doing what I do as unto the Lord means doing my work so it has quality."

Telva Urban says she believes that the quality of her work speaks a faith message much more forcefully than any overt evangelism. "I try to do my best," she says, "and I see that as a service to God. I've worked with a few Christian nurses who viewed their job as their mission field—and I didn't quite go along with the program on that because they were trying to evangelize instead of do their job. I remember one woman who would go and pray with her patients before she did anything else, and then she'd get behind in her medications and would go running around asking everyone else for help. I've consciously avoided that. My faith just motivates me to do the best job I can and not take shortcuts."

Expressing Faith through Relationships

As an executive for a company that publishes Sunday-school curricula, Marlene LeFever is able to express her faith very directly in the content of her work. But, as she points out, "Companies aren't Christian. People are." Marlene believes that a more important expression of her faith is the way she treats her customers and her coworkers.

"I am a very product-centered person," she says. "I know deadlines. I write things on paper. I enjoy getting things done. For someone like me, the biggest challenge is to care more about the people who are putting out the product than the product itself.

"It's a constant hassle for me to make sure that I care about what's happening in my associates' lives, that I take time to listen. One of my associates' in-laws was in the Philippines when the earthquake happened. Now my desk is piled up like a great little pyramid, yet my coworker's concerns were more important than getting my stuff out on time. It's an indication of Christ's love through me to her if I'm able to sit and listen and talk. That doesn't come naturally to me.

"I had one employee tell me how much he resented coming into my office, speaking to me about something that was very important to him and having me answer every telephone call that came through while he was sitting there. The implicit message was, whoever is calling is more important than he is. He taught me something. Since then, I don't answer the telephone when someone is in my office because I want to show them that as a manager, as a Christian, I care.

"Just being in a Christian company doesn't make us Christian in our relationships with others—that's work. It's difficult to deal with failure in a Christian company. How do you fire someone in a Christian way? I really believe it can be done. How do you tell someone, 'This is a schlocky job, it's not good enough' without saying, 'You are a schlocky person and not good enough'? I've done it poorly and I've done it superbly.

"When I'm speaking at a Sunday-school convention and I'm dead tired and somebody comes up with tears in their eyes and says, 'I need help,' as a task-oriented person my tendency is to think, 'I'm sorry, I've done my thing here, I can't move, please let me go back to my room and collapse.' But as a representative of Christ, I don't have that option. I really don't. It's my responsibility to respond in love and to say, 'Yeah. Let's talk. Let's pray.'

"Then there are the relationships with our customers. We sell curriculum. That's how we make a living. So it's important for us to be out there saying, 'We've got a product we think you need.' But it's also important for me to be honest about it. When someone asks, 'What do you have in the cradle roll area?' I have to say, 'Well, not much, but we're working on it.' Or if I'm asked, 'What's the difference between your product and other independent publishers?' how do I answer that question? I can answer it in a non-Christian way—lambast everything I can think of about our competitors. Or I can answer in a Christian way—present the points that I think are valid for us and never cut down the competition.

"For me, expressing my faith in my work means modeling myself after Christ in my relationships, asking myself what Christ would do in a particular situation."

Businessman Ken Smith testifies to the change that the faith variable has made in his work relationships: "Before I became a Christian," he recalls, "I knew enough to treat people civilly, but it was only so they could contribute something to me. I never thought about what I could contribute to them. The Lord changed all that. So I think that your contacts in business—the way you care about others—is one of the first expressions of Christianity in the workplace. It sure ought to be a characteristic of God's people that they have a concern for people around them.

"I would hate to hear," he continues, "that people in this company are saying that, as head of the company, I take advantage of them or don't care about them. I hope that I'm able to show that I care about their problems. I don't mean that it's appropriate to be a busybody in everybody's affairs, but there are times you can be an encouragement and you ought to be. That includes fairness, seeking the other person's benefit—what the Scripture refers to as love."

Expressing Faith in the Act of Creation

For many work lovers, the very act of working is an act of faith because it allows them to imitate the creativity of God. "Imagination is part of how faith interacts with work," says Martin Marty. "I have apprehended, grasped, critiqued and taught a doctrine of creation—*creatio continua* rather than *creatio ex nihilo*. Creation out of nothing is not taught in the Bible, but I think it squares with the Bible. The Bible, however, stresses that God is bringing order out of chaos. We get to participate in the act. I think that anyone who gets to use words, either orally or in writing or in teaching, is in some way a creative artist who gets to participate in creation, in the act of imagination."

Expressing Faith in the Results of Work

Work can be an expression of faith both in its process, and in its results. Many work lovers cite the results of their work as both evidence of spiritual validity and cause for satisfaction.

Businessman Gary Ginter says that one important result of spiritually valid work—and one cause of work satisfaction—is what he calls "enablement." "When you work in a complex financial services industry, as I do," he says, "you have to ask yourself, 'Does my work really contribute to the production of goods and services that are beneficial to people? Does it benefit society or only small segments of society? Does the process of doing your work enable the stakeholders involved—you, your employer, your peers, your customers, your suppliers?'

"Enablement is defined by the person involved," he continues. "If I were working with a Christian brother or sister, then I would use words like this, 'I want our interaction to enable you to be better able to respond to the call of God as you interpret it.' But whether or not I'm working with someone who shares my faith, enablement is a meaningful concept, so long as I negotiate the shape of enablement. It could be defined in terms of job challenge, responsibilities, authority, scope, remuneration, status or title. You can't seek to impose your definition of enablement on someone else, but a quick test of whether work is enabling is this: Is this pleasing to God? Is it other-directed? Is it bottom-up rather than top-down? Is it reciprocal?

"Enablement is somewhat about money, but not just about money. Like right livelihood, it is a wholistic concept which embodies the ideas, flavor and tonal quality of shalom in the Old Testament. It means justice at the level of economics, but also peace and right relationships."

When some work lovers talk about expressing their faith through the results of their work, they talk in terms of service. Dr. Ken Phillips: "I grew up believing that I was put on the earth for a purpose to do good in the sense that Christ did good—laying down his life for others, caring for others, lifting people up. I don't pretend that what I do is sacrificial service because I get paid well. But I have a continual sense on a certain level that this is ministry, that I get to help people in a very direct way. For me, there is a spiritual dimension. And I have to have that because from my earliest teenage years I've wondered about a call to ministry."

Expressing Faith through Obedience to God's Call
Pastoral counselor David Hogue didn't set out to be a therapist. He

responded to what he believed was God's call to ministry and eventually focused his ministry on pastoral counseling. Unlike some of his peers, however, he still feels that he is called to be a pastor first and counselor second. For David, his work is an expression of faith to the degree that represents a continued response to his call. "I still feel strongly that my main call is to be a pastor," he says. "I think that's why I've resisted licensure. I have the training and I could get it, but it starts confusing my identity. I don't want to be called a psychologist. I'd like the benefits—higher pay, the ability to sign for insurance forms—but it's not what I am. It's very important to me that what I'm doing is consistent with my calling."

Expressing Faith by Using Your Gifts

Jim Steere never received a call to ministry, and he spent years feeling guilty about it. With a pastor father and missionary grandparents, he grew up with the expectation that he would follow in the footsteps of his forebears. "I've really struggled with it," confides Jim, who eventually followed his dream and became a photographer. "It's only been in the last four years or so that I've felt it's okay to be something other than a pastor or missionary. I finally came to grips with the fact that God can be glorified in anything you do if you understand who you are and how God made you—if you don't try to be something you think God wants you to be or something somebody told you God wants you to be. You can work to the glory of God by taking your gifts and skills and using them to the best of your ability."

College president David Horner echoes that belief: "Apart from the mission of the organization I serve, the faith basis for my work is incorporated in the fact that it is an expression of who God created me to be," he says. "I have a sense that while I don't do it ever perfectly or totally faithfully, to the degree that I understand what God has given me to work with, I'm working with it here."

Work as Part of a Life of Faith

"My work stems out of my spiritual journey," says author Karen Mains. "Authenticity in my personal life is the most important thing in Christian expression."

For Karen Mains and many other work lovers, work is an expression of faith in the same way that all other aspects of life are an expression of faith. Work, family, recreation—they are all part of a seamless spiritual journey.

Ron Nikkel, president of Prison Fellowship International, explains: "If I look at my vocation in the largest possible sense—living out the life of Christ—I can't really separate the work I'm doing and my everyday relationships and other activities," he says. "It's all ministry. It's all spiritual. It's all part and parcel of the same thing."

Satisfaction Is Having a Spiritual Vocation

For people of faith who love their work, it's important that work, like the rest of their lives, be an expression of their relationship to God and of who God created them to be. Whether their faith is expressed in the motivation for their work, the content of their work, the manner of their work or the quality of their work— whether they seek to glorify God through caring work relationships, through imitation of God's creativity, through obedience to God's call or through use of God-given gifts—work lovers enjoy the satisfaction of knowing that their work is more than just a collection of tasks, even if they're enjoyable tasks. For these people, work is an expression of a spiritual vocation.

If you've found work that you enjoy, but see no connection between it and your faith, take another look. You don't have to be in the ministry or on the mission field to have a spiritual vocation. If you're doing what God created you to do, your work is a direct expression of faith. And, more often than not, that makes it easy to love.

11

Finding the Right Place

Listening for God's voice . . .
Finding models and mentors . . .
Discovering your gifted passions . . .
Taking risks . . .
Making sacrifices . . .
Expressing your faith . . .
Earning enough money . . .
Developing competence . . .
Finding community . . .

You can do all the right things and still not love your work if you're doing it in the wrong place. Just ask church music director John Folkening.

John knew what he wanted to do with his life by the time he reached eighth grade. "It was pretty nice," he recalls. "While other kids were struggling with vocational choices, I just said, 'I know what I want to do. I want to be a church organist and choir director and teach at a Lutheran school.' " He never even considered other vocational options.

Fortunately, John's gifts supported his ambitions. It was clear early on that he had a talent for music. He could sing harmony and play the piano pretty well by the fifth grade—and was already playing the organ in church by the time he was in seventh grade. The regular organist let him play while he went to the altar for communion. John was extremely proud of the fact that he could put his hand under the organist's hand while he was holding a chord—and continue playing without a break. "That was considered really wonderful," laughs John. "In fact, my mother's greatest compliment to me was, 'John, I couldn't even tell when you got on the organ.' I was in absolute heaven.' "

Buoyed by that kind of encouragement, John forged ahead with his vocational decision. After graduating from high school, he attended a Lutheran teacher's college, earned bachelor's and master's degrees and then landed a job as a Lutheran school teacher/ choir director/church organist.

He'd achieved his dream. But he soon realized he wasn't enjoying it as much as he thought he would. He was doing everything he'd expected to do—teaching academic subjects half a day, teaching music the other half, directing the choir and playing the organ—but something wasn't quite right. He got a clue about what it was when he went back to his alma mater for an annual conference on church music.

"I got all these neat ideas but I couldn't use them because the pastor simply wasn't interested," recalls John. "For him, the high point of the church service was the sermon. Anything else was subservient. He seemed to view the choir as an intrusion. Plus, the principal of the school viewed music as a luxury and whenever there were budget problems, the music program was the first thing to be cut."

Despite his dissatisfactions, John stayed on for nine years. But when he got a call asking if he'd like to be considered for a position at a church near Chicago, he jumped at the chance.

John got the job and came to work at Grace Lutheran Church in River Forest, Illinois, where he now serves as music director. "I came here with a little bit of fear and trembling," remembers John, "because there was a tradition of excellent music and the people had very high standards. I could see that I'd been lagging far behind in what I'd been doing. But there were some wonderful advantages I'd never had before—wonderful acoustics, a good pipe organ, a pastor who was very supportive of the music program and who saw me as a co-minister. Above all, the pastor and the people saw worship as the real focal point of the congregational life. For me, it was the difference between night and day.

"This place has been the biggest affirmation that what I'm doing is the right direction for me to go," he continues. "My biggest joy is to look at the lessons for each Sunday and to see what they hold musically and creatively for the resources I have here. I definitely feel that it was God who led me here."

For John Folkening, finding the right place to exercise his gifts made the difference between being frustrated with work and loving his work. For him, finding the right place meant finding the right employer. The same is true for many work lovers:

☐ Richard Blackburn, high-school English teacher: The day I came to interview at this school was one of the highlights of my life. I went home so sky high I turned down a full-time offer at another school to take a one-semester job here. It's exciting to work here with a staff of teachers who go off and win grants to do summer research, people who write their own textbooks, people who could do a thousand other things but chose to teach. Our department chair, a real intellectual cheerleader, said once that her job here is like managing the great singers in the Metropolitan Opera. It's a pleasure to be in this tremendously stimulating environment.

☐ Dale Bonga, securities broker: I really feel blessed to be with a firm like the one I'm with now, a firm that doesn't take risks. Because I don't need to be with a firm that takes risks to serve my clients well. Sometimes it takes you longer in life to figure out what you really need. The things that some of my previous firms did were very risky, and consequently they no longer exist today. I don't need a firm that bets all the capital every day.

☐ Tim Botts, graphic designer: Even though you don't hear much about this anymore, I feel I was called to Tyndale House. Everything came together in such a way that I felt very strongly that God was leading me there. I haven't felt a call since then to anywhere else.

☐ David Horner, college president: To be very happy, I've got to respect the institution for which I'm working. A professor of mine at Stanford said, "There's really only one person who has to believe all the public relations stuff about a school and that's the president. If the president doesn't really believe it, you're in trouble." One of the institutions I used to head really tested me. I loved the place, but there were things I felt were just not strong enough that didn't get fixed quickly enough. So place is very important to me in that way.

☐ Marlene LeFever, writer/publishing executive: Place is extremely important. This company has been incredibly kind in looking at who I am as a person, seeing what my strong points are and then building a job description around the needs of the company but also the strong points of me. If I were to leave, the job description would probably change because it is so completely "Marlene." I could not work anywhere else. I get job offers from other places. I used to look at them carefully. Now I look at them and I'm flattered that they asked. It would be very, very difficult for me to leave this company.

☐ Kevin Miller, magazine editor: I derive a feeling of satisfaction and status from this organization. I feel the people I work with are good at what they do, are pleasant to work with and have integrity. I don't have to be embarrassed about practices that are going on here. I feel good about the way people are managed. I derive satisfaction from the fact that our periodicals regularly win awards, that they are read. So that's satisfying.

☐ Pat Reinhofer, executive secretary: Before I came to work here, I worked for six months for a union. I just hated it. There was nothing to do. I hated having to sit there, trying to look busy. My boss said, "What would it look like if we told the New York office we didn't have enough work for two secretaries?" Plus, there was some rumor of scandal. I was just happy to get out of there. But I like working for a social service agency because people have a whole different attitude. They're really dedicated and they're not worrying about profits all the time. They're all caring people. I think we have one of the best alcohol and drug dependence programs around.

While some work lovers find their place in congenial organizations, others speak of the importance of finding the right community, or physical environment or, in the case of artists, genre:

☐ Ann Anderson, mother: I couldn't be happy raising my children just anywhere. I can't even imagine what it would be like to worry about the safety of your children when they walk out the door. I can't imagine what it must be like not to be able to keep your house clean. It's a different proposition for people who are faced with those limitations than it is for someone who lives in a neighborhood like this. I don't have to be in this particular neighborhood to be happy, although the fact that we're raising our children close to our family has a big impact on our lives. My son Joseph gets daily phone calls from his uncle, who just loves him. He's with my parents frequently and they love him. His best friends are his cousins. He loves being with his cousins more than Disneyland or Kiddieland or anything. So it's hard to overestimate the importance of the people who are associated with this place. We are extraordinarily blessed to be able to raise our children in this kind of setting.

☐ Elizabeth Cody Newenhuyse, author/journalist: Place is very important to me. I really like staying in one place. I find if I've been traveling, I enjoy it, but then I get really drained. For me, a certain rootedness inspires creativity. When certain things are in order, I'm freed to see more deeply.

☐ Rich Berg, bond salesman: For me, it was very important to find the right place to get into sales. I knew I could sell, but I didn't want to use that gift to manipulate people, which is what I thought sales was about. I was offered a job selling copiers, but I don't think I would have resigned my teaching position to do that. People don't want to see you and you've gotta sell them anyway—that didn't appeal to me. But this business was intriguing to me. It combines both sales and finance which, as a math major, was interesting to me. Still, it took me awhile to come to the point where I could say, "This is not what I thought sales was about. This is a worthwhile occupation, I can have fun at it, and I can make money at it."

☐ Karen Mains, author: My place has been evangelicalism. It's home territory. I'm restless in it now, but I'm not negative about it. I'm very, very grateful that it gave me a place and allowed me to develop. But it wasn't my true emotional home. I'm finding now that I need the true creative forms. I'm writing a novel, for example, and I have a script making the rounds in Hollywood. In a way, I hope the script doesn't go because I can't see them doing it the way I want, but I'm finding that I get great satisfaction in this. I've started to feel that I've come into my true home territory—almost as though I've gone through most of my adult life speaking a second language and suddenly I'm speaking my primary language. I don't have to transliterate anymore. So in a way, evangelicalism has been the home of a displaced person. But I'm very grateful for the foster parenting.

Work lovers are people who have discovered what kind of place nurtures their love of their work. For some people, the right place means the right organization. For others, it means the right geographical setting, or community, or industry, or group of people. Someone else's wrong place may be the right place for you and vice versa. But if you can find your place—often a trial-and-error process—you'll have found one of the secrets of loving your work.

12

Achieving Balance

IF YOU'RE DOING THE WORK YOU LOVE YOU'LL WANT TO DO IT ALL THE time. Right?

Not necessarily.

Some work lovers *are* single-focus zealots whose passion for the work they love leaves little room in their lives for other interests. But most people who love their work say their lives are characterized by what they believe is a healthy degree of balance.

Almost all the work lovers I talked to agreed that balance is important in order to continue loving their work. For some work lovers, however, achieving balance can be something of a struggle:

☐ Greg Darnieder, executive director, inner-city tutoring ministry: My wife and I used to joke about my not taking vacations—our one vacation was to Joliet [an industrial town about thirty miles outside the city where Greg works]. So we really took a look at that, and about two months ago, for the first time in sixteen years, we took a vacation for a week. Some friends lent us their house in Florida. It was the first time since we were married we'd ever been alone for any period of time. That was a real healthy experience. It showed us the importance of balancing our lives. Time is a precious commodity, but God took a seventh day of rest. So how am I going to integrate that in my life? Is it literally just about Sunday or does it mean something else—something about taking care of yourself and being healthy mentally as well as physically?

☐ Barb Daly, corporate trainer: I have to force myself to have balance, but I think balance is better. I enjoy eating at restaurants and going to bookstores. When I have what I consider to be a good day, I've probably been to eight bookstores. And for the past fifteen years, church has helped me to be organized about keeping balance in my life. I think the reason I keep balanced is because I see it pays off.

☐ Elizabeth Cody Newenhuyse, author/journalist: I would like my life to be more balanced. I'm double-focused on my work and my home and family. What I struggle with is wanting more time to nurture friendships, more church involvement and volunteering for a worthy cause. Having said that, I do have a rather pleasant, orderly, satisfying kind of life. We decided to buy a house near my office so I don't have a lengthy commute every day. I'm home by three so I can be with my daughter. We have a garden I can putter around in. Our parents live in the area so we enjoy the pleasure of an extended family. I couldn't be one of those workaholic, always-at-the-office types you hear about. I've realized that I'm a person who needs a certain amount of "creative lassitude" to really thrive.

☐ Ron Nikkel, president, international prison ministry: My vocation is a kind of passion, and there's a danger that comes with that of becoming so focused on the mission that there isn't balance. There are times when I get too focused and almost burned out from what I'm doing, not to the point where I want out, but to the point where my work is so all-consuming that other relationships suffer as a consequence, that I don't pay as much attention to my physical well-being as I should, I don't exercise properly or I work when I ought to be relaxing. Canoeing and hiking are strong interests of mine that I don't indulge as much as I would like. I used to have a pretty decent balance between the activist part of my life and the more contemplative part. I used to take a week every quarter to go to a monastery for a period of reflection and meditation and spiritual renewal. I haven't done that for a few years, so if there's any part of my life that's suffered in the midst of activism it's the inward side. There is such a thing as the spirituality of service, but I think sometimes you need to get far enough away from the noise of it that you can hear God speak.

☐ Chuck Swirsky, sports broadcaster: My work is my consuming passion, but I force myself to do other things because if I didn't I'd turn into a vegetable. I make chocolate chip cookies, I enjoy going to the theater and I love music. I write poetry. Being married, with a newborn baby, I'm working at balancing things out.

Work lovers differ in the ease with which they achieve balance—as well as the *way* in which they achieve it. Some find balance outside of work—in family or hobbies or volunteer activities. Some find it in the variety of their work itself. Still others find that, while they cannot be balanced at all times in their work lives, they can achieve what might be called a "serial" balance in the seasons of their lives.

The majority of work lovers I talked with said they found balance in activities outside their work:

☐ Ann Anderson, mother: I'm most focused on raising my children, but both my husband and I have many interests, almost too many interests to manage comfortably. We are both avid musicians and music lovers and that's a big part of our lives. I like to paint. I love to do needlework and sewing and stitching and anything with a needle. I absolutely insist on making time for that and feel very aggravated and annoyed when I don't have time for it. Right now, my great passionate hobby is making clothes for my kids. I love to smock and so I'm able to have an excuse for my stitching.

☐ Peter Baker, pediatrician: I have several abiding interests outside of work. One is community theater. About once a year I put my ego on the line and try out for a play. I also read history which is really a joy. And I love gardening. It's very satisfying to see things grow, to see delicate little plants make it. Each of these other interests is so different from the practice of medicine that they make a wonderful change of pace. I don't think I could be an all-absorbed, intense-every-minute-about-my-profession kind of person. I really need these other blocks of time to do something different.

☐ Rich Blackburn, high-school English teacher: Teaching is a wonderful profession for hobbies. We have a faculty softball team named "The Naturals" after the Robert Redford film. We challenge senior jocks from the high-school football, basketball and baseball teams. We knock heads with these guys, and we've won seventy-five to eighty per cent of our games. I'm also active musically, singing and playing instruments. Two summers ago, to celebrate getting my masters' degree, I did nothing academic over summer—I just went out and rented a euphonium and practiced up again. And my latest hobby is my children—Kate, who's going to be five, and Anne, who's five months.. Marriage and child-raising takes a lot of time but it's a riot. I also enjoy hiking and climbing and doing poetry about climbing.

☐ Dale Bonga, securities broker: I think the person who can't get away from his work is out of control. The older I get, the more my interest is my family. Three of my kids play basketball, and I had seventy basketball games to attend one season. One week, we went to fourteen basketball events, eight of which I coached. I left early a few days to do it, because that's a priority for me.

☐ John Folkening, church music director: I don't do a lot in the way of hobbies, but since my wife has gone back to full-time teaching, I'm sharing a lot of the roles she did at home. I'm cooking more meals, for example, and I get as much enjoyment out of that as any hobby. Plus, the kids get to see that Dad doesn't just work at church. I think that balance is important. I'm not consumed by what I do to the point that I can't let it go.

☐ Dave Himelick, carpenter/building contractor: I try to make work real important for five days a week and then the other two days I think should be spent on other things. I like to golf and ski, and I'd like to start doing woodworking as a hobby. I like my work but I see the need for drawing the line at a certain level so it's not all-consuming. My partner started out working six days a week and he almost burned out. I told him he had to stop. Work is important but you have to be balanced or you'll burn out.

☐ David Orth, woodworker: I think running your own business makes you more obsessive about work than most people with nine-to-five jobs, but you have to have balance. I find that I really only want to do this part of the time. I like my work too much to want to burn myself out. Spending time with my wife doing things together, reading, going to church, playing my guitar, spending time with friends—these are all real important balances for me. I would find it exhausting if everything in my life was woodworking.

☐ Pat Reinhofer, executive secretary: I have a lot of interests besides work. Today I rode nineteen miles on a bike path with my brother. I like all sports, as long as I can participate. I don't like sitting and watching somebody else do it. I read. I sing in a 100-voice chorus. Work isn't my whole life. It's one element of my life that gives me pleasure.

If vocation has to do with how you use your gifts in the entire shape of your life, rather than just in the hours for which you get paid, it can be difficult to separate work from the activities that balance work. But sometimes it is possible to find balance within work itself, as pastor Melicent Huneycutt has discovered. "My work is so varied," she says. "It has everything. It has counseling. It has recreation built in because I build social opportunities for other people to build fellowship for them. It has time for study and quietness and reflection and meditation built in. It has public times and private times. I guess I'm so immersed in community that it's almost impossible for me at any stage of my life to say this is my private life and this is my public life. Or this is my job and this is not my job. And I find it satisfying because it's so varied. It's just a matter of pacing and paying attention so I don't do too much of the same kind of thing end to end and back to back."

If you tallied up all of Marlene LeFever's activities, you'd conclude that she leads a very balanced life, until you understand that most of her activities are work-focused. But perhaps there's a certain balance in that. "I'm a reader," she says. "I play racquetball. I entertain a lot. If I listed all the things I do, it sounds like, oh, well, a pretty full life. But it all centers around the whole communication of Christian education. Very little in my life is outside that. I play racquetball so I don't get a backache when I come in the office to write my articles. I entertain because I have a book on the subject and it's fun for my husband to do, and I always keep notes in case I ever want to use them in an article. So everything centers around the core of what I believe is my talent area

—speaking, writing, teaching."

Admonitions to live a balanced life can be terribly guilt-producing for people who are sacrificing time and money and recreation to pursue the work they love. For the medical student, the entrepreneur just starting a business, or the mother of a newborn, the ideal of a balanced life may appear to be a cruel mirage. But if balance is impossible at this stage of life, you don't necessarily have to despair. Sometimes it's possible to balance the seasons of your life.

Psychiatrist Ken Phillips: "I'm a pretty firm believer in different seasons for different emphases. It's a pretty difficult thing, if you have a career that involves a lot of investment, to keep a balance all the way through. When I was in medical school, it was pretty darn hard to be balanced. There were a few people who said, 'Okay, I've got my studies, I've got my quiet time, I've got my personal exercise, I have my friends, and oh, yes, I'm involved in the church.' But that was pretty rare. What I think is more common—and maybe not necessarily bad—is to be a little out of balance for awhile to accomplish a task. Someone may say, 'I've got to go through boot camp in order to get into the Marine Corps and I won't see my family for awhile and I may not go to church for eight weeks, but I have a purpose in mind.' I think that makes sense as long as I don't lose my internal balance or my ability to come back into balance. I hope that's not a rationalization. Fortunately, my life is more in balance now—which is great! I've got time to go to church twice a week. I've got time to play with my son and I go out and play golf. But if I had limited myself to fifty or sixty hours a week while I was in training, I probably wouldn't be a very good psychiatrist.

The danger of serial balance, of course, is the temptation to perpetually postpone. "As soon as I finish school . . . get my promotion . . . complete this project . . . I'll start living a more balanced life." For some people, the season for balance never comes. And yet others manage to achieve balance despite heavy demands and hectic schedules.

Because of his extraordinary productivity, few people would hold it against church historian Martin Marty if he were to confess to a lack of balance between work and other aspects of his life. A much-in-demand professor, author, speaker and editor, he could easily fill his days with nothing but work. There are some who think that's exactly what he does. But despite the opinions of observers, he believes his life is balanced:

"I read a story about a Mennonite who was asked, 'Are you a Christian?' And he said, 'I'll give you a list of five people who can't stand me and five people who like me and you listen to all of them and decide whether or not I'm a Christian.' If you ask me if my life is balanced, I should give you a list of five names and tell you to find out. But I disagree with some of the perceptions of me. In my perception, my wife and I goof off a lot. She and I walk in the streets of the town. We see a reasonable number of plays. Our hobby is going out with or taking people out to eat just to pass a few hours of conversation. I do have a lot of energy and I put in long days. I started at five this morning, and then at four o'clock this afternoon the doorbell rang. I'd been writing all that time, but it seemed like two hours. Tonight I'll do some proofreading, we'll take our walk, we'll have a relaxed dinner and we'll shop for an hour. Because I put in long days, it looks like a lot of work.

"I make a distinction between being busy and being scheduled," he says. "Some people can't prevent being busy in their work because other people make demands. If I set my own schedule and I'm busy, there's something wrong. Busy means I've lost control. Occupied is worse—I have no time for you, I have no time for my wife—I'm occupied. I'm *not* busy, I'm *not* occupied—but I *am* scheduled. I think that every Thursday through the next year is scheduled. I speak somewhere every Thursday. Some people come along and say, 'Oh, man, Marty's busy!' No! I'll read Wednesday night. I'll read on the airplane on my way to a lecture at Vassar. I'll insist on not having breakfast with people so I can have some hours in the hotel room in the morning. Then I'll knock myself out till the end of the lecture. I'll have dinner with my host. I'll have read four hours in the room that Vassar gave me. That's scheduled life. I think that's one thing that allows me to lead a more balanced life than most people think I lead. I don't feel stressed. I don't feel overworked. There are times when so many demands are made that I have empathy with people who do feel stressed and over-worked, but I'm philosophically committed to balance."

After talking with work lovers who say their lives are balanced as well as those who say theirs aren't, I've come to this conclusion: It's possible to love your work without balancing it with recreation and family and other aspects of life, but balance makes it a lot easier to love your entire *life*. So if you want to love your work in the context of your whole life, look for ways to find balance. If there's a sport, hobby or avocation that energizes rather than de-pletes you, be intentional about making room for it in your life. If, in the quest for balance, you take up an activity and find that it becomes just another task to check off your list, find something else.

Instead of taking up a lot of new activities, look for ways to create more time for the nonwork-related aspects of your life—even if they don't fit into the category of recreation. Hanging out with your family, cooking, fixing up the house, washing the car—just accom-plishing the activities of daily living without the frenzy that char-acterizes so much of modern life can contribute to your overall sense of balance.

Nurture the contemplative side of yourself. Read books. Take time to do nothing. Go on a retreat. Pray. Cultivate your inner life.

If you're in the sacrificial stage of your work right now, try to make your work itself as varied as possible. And make sure there's a light at the end of the tunnel—if you can't foresee a time when you'll ever be able to be balanced, perhaps you're pursuing the wrong kind of work or the right kind of work in the wrong environment.

Balance doesn't necessarily come easily. But most work lovers believe in it and strive to achieve it. They may struggle. They may find it in different ways. But most of them find it, even if it takes them years to do it.

13

Believing
Your Work Is
Important

When I've met people who really love their work,
they're usually people who say two things about it:
"I can do it well and I think it's important."

BARBARA DALY,
CORPORATE TRAINER

THE FIRST TIME IT OCCURRED TO ME THAT IT IS CRUCIAL TO BELIEVE
your work is important was when I was standing in line at a phar-
macy. The pharmacist, a middle-aged man with a dignified, almost
courtly manner, was waiting on a seemingly endless stream of customers, most of whom appeared to be buying over-the-counter cold
remedies. It struck me that this man, who had undergone rigorous
training in the finer points of pharmaceuticals, was spending most
of his time punching a cash register and making change. In my
mind, it would have been understandable if he had thought to
himself, *I spent all those years training to be a pharmacist and here I am*
peddling aspirins and nasal spray—doing a job any clerk could do. But
he showed no sign of that attitude. Instead, he treated each transaction as if it were of infinite importance. What's more, he seemed
to be genuinely enjoying himself.

That incident stuck in my mind and reinforced a growing impression as I encountered other people who seemed to enjoy their work. That impression, which has now become a conviction, is this: People who love their work are people who have an unusual ability to find importance in their work.

Ron Nikkel, a ruddy, bear-like man in his late forties, is president of Prison Fellowship International. As a self-described minister of reconciliation within the criminal justice system, he travels all over the world seeking to bring peace and restoration into broken relationships—relationships between prisoners and other prisoners, between prisoners and the community, between prisoners and their victims, and between prisoners and their families. He loves his work more than almost anyone I know. And as much as anyone I've ever met, he believes his work is important. Although normally a reserved, almost taciturn man, when asked to explain why his work is so important, he responds with eagerness and the kind of multiplicity of words that grows out of deep conviction.

"If there is a single strategic place where the truth of Christianity can be demonstrated, it's in the criminal justice system," he says. "It's a place where individuals have failed and where society has failed.

"The individuals can't do anything to help themselves. And it's becoming increasingly evident that society can't do anything to change the criminal personality, the character of fallen man. But I can tell you numerous stories of hard-core offenders who suddenly encounter Christ and everything is different—in a way that is not explainable in human terms.

"I remember talking with the Inspector General of Prisons in one of the states of India who, even though he was a Brahmin Hindu, was absolutely fascinated with the Prison Fellowship program in his state. He told me, 'I have been in charge of prisons here for more than twenty years. Some of the prisoners have been here as long as I have. Many of them are in and out of prisons all the time. Nothing changes them. And then suddenly in come a few Christians and everything is changed.'

"The criminal justice system is the most difficult place in society. If something works there, it's bound to have a profound impact. But the only thing that works is the power of Christ. So the church ought to be there."

Who could doubt, after hearing these words, that Ron Nikkel believes his work is important?

The value of Ron's work in the criminal justice system is plain to see, especially when you consider the results. But often, work lovers are able to see value and meaning where other people don't.

I was surprised, during a trip to China in 1981, when our government-appointed guide proudly pointed out the free markets where farmers could sell their own produce and keep the profits. Isn't that capitalism, my companions and I asked? No, insisted the guide, suddenly stern, because there are no middlemen. We have no *speculators* in China.

Speculator. For some, the word is synonymous with the worst excesses of the capitalistic system. When asked to free-associate about speculators, for example, my officemates reacted with curled lips: "Ruthless." "Gamblers." "Shady characters." "Car salesman types."

Based on the characterizations of these people-down-the-hall, you'd think that as a species, speculators should occupy a place very low on the scale of life forms. Obviously, in the eyes of many, the work of speculators is not only unimportant, but contemptible—of negative value.

These people undoubtedly haven't met Gary Ginter. Gary, one of the founding partners of an extremely successful commodities trading firm, is, in a sense, a speculator. He is also an intensely spiritual man and a passionate work lover. And like most work lovers I've talked to, he fervently believes that his work is very important, that it's worth doing. Hear his impassioned defense of the practical results of his work.

"Speculators represent a net benefit to society," he argues. "They only make money if they buy something that would have been too cheap in the long run or sell something that would have been too dear in the long run. The effect of a successful speculation is to bring prices closer to where they should have been. So speculation improves the accuracy of price signals in the economy.

"People in general do better when the economy in general is more efficient and coordinated and finely tuned," he continues. "But people overlook the foundational importance of speculation in helping the price discovery process."

The societal benefit of his work is only one evidence that it is important, says Gary. Another is the fact that it generates a profit. "Making a profit is the best evidence that what you're doing is worth doing in terms of the marketplace," he explains. "In business, if you're not making profit, the market is telling you that what you're doing isn't worth doing.

"But I don't care if I make a lot of money or a little money," he admits. "Making a whole bunch of money isn't as interesting as whether or not you benefitted the people you did it with, whether you're fully growing into the kind of person you're trying to become, whether you're overcoming weakness, whether you're becoming a more complete and mature adult, whether you're overcoming the wounded child we all are when we start. That's what business does when it's good."

Above all, says Gary, his work is important because it isn't just work. To him, it's a vocation. A right livelihood. A calling.

"I think we need to go back to Calvin and Luther and recapture the concept of *vocatio,* the calling of God to the people of God to do the work of God in the world," he says. "To me, vocation is authentic when it enables you to express your giftedness, when it's consonant with God's purposes in the world and when it's in sync with what God is up to in your time and the place he's put you."

Gary believes his work is a true vocation because it fits his gifts and because it offers him the opportunity to "demonstrate kingdom life in a fallen world."

"My work fits my gifts beautifully," he explains. "I find what I do is very easy because it's such a natural expression of how God put me together."

What Gary doesn't explain, but his friends attest to, is the degree to which he "demonstrates kingdom life in a fallen world." By his own definition that means "the way you live is radically different." As someone who has made huge sums of money, but kept little of it for himself, Gary Ginter is clearly a businessman who lives in a radically different way. Ultimately, Gary's work is a true vocation because he has been called to do it. "I could enjoy a lot of different fields," he says, "but it just so happens that the mundane details of business form the arena into which God has called me."

God had to call Gary into business, because he never would have considered it on his own. "My dad had been an entrepreneur and it wasn't all easy street," Gary explains. "I was born in one of his down cycles and business stole my childhood. So I didn't want to be an entrepreneur. Instead, I went to Bible school, intending to be a missionary. But in my second year, God made it clear that he was calling me into business. I experienced firsthand what the apostle Paul talks about when he says God is at work to will and do his own good pleasure. He had to do that with me because I had no interest in business. But God worked it out so that I also enjoyed my work—it gives me a pleasure that continues to this day."

Gary loves his work in part because he believes it is important. The same is true of most people who love their work. Regardless of how others may view what they do, work lovers have found meaning and value in their work. Why? For some of the same reasons articulated by Gary Ginter.

They're Meeting a Need

It's been said that the secret to success is finding a need and filling it. It may also be one of the secrets to loving your work. When you know your work is meeting a need, you tend to believe it's important. And believing your work is important is almost always a prerequisite to deriving deep satisfaction in doing it.

Meeting a need was a strong basis of satisfaction for these work lovers:

☐ Barbara Daly, corporate trainer: If I do my job right, it's going to make life easier and simpler for the people I work with. And it's important to me to be doing something that helps.

☐ Kurt Neradt, dry wall taper: Tapers are one of the cogs in one of the wheels of construction. We're a piece of the puzzle. Without us, one of the pieces wouldn't be there.

☐ Chuck Swirsky, sports announcer: The Chicago Cubs can't stop a world crisis, but people can come to the ballpark and forget what's going on, whether they're having marital problems, family crises, or a tough day at the office. They can go to the ball game and clear their minds for a couple of hours. I think that's a benefit to our society.

☐ Jim Steere, photographer: I like the fact that people choose to use my skills because it helps them accomplish their ends. That's probably the most satisfying thing about my work. I do catalog photos for a company that sells little knickknacks, for example, and I'm glad to work for them because, even though it may not seem very important to other people, it's important to them.

☐ Ann Anderson, mother: Someone has to raise children. There's so much talk now about what's going to happen to our society with most children being raised by people who aren't their parents. So my work is important because people are important.

☐ Rich Blackburn, English teacher: A friend of mine who used to be with the FBI said his main complaint was that his agents, college graduates who became special agents with the FBI, couldn't write a report. People have to learn how to communicate in complete understandable ways. Kids have to learn how to mean what they say and write what they mean. So my work is of the utmost importance.

☐ David Horner, college president: This work is important, not because I'm doing it, but because I'm a true believer in the value of education generally and Christian higher education in particular. I feel it made a huge contribution in my life and I've seen it help lots of students along the way.

☐ Kevin Miller, editor, *Christian History* magazine: There are many Christians who want to know about church history and would benefit from it, but they don't have time to read a 300-page, heavily footnoted volume on a single slice of history. But they will read fifty colorfully illustrated pages of prose that has some verve and vitality. So I feel like I'm broadening people's world views, and that's terribly important.

☐ Telva Urban, dialysis nurse: My work is important because the people I work with will die if they don't have dialysis.

☐ Calvin Long, math professor: Mathematics is critically important to modern life. You can hardly read a newspaper intelligently without an understanding of math. And I believe many of our policymakers are making poor decisions because they don't understand the numbers behind them.

☐ Ken Phillips, psychiatrist: My work is magnificently important. What, besides your eternal destiny, could be more important than how you experience life and yourself? It's where the rubber meets the road.

They're Gratified by the Response to Their Work

Like the pharmacist dispensing nasal spray as if it were a revolutionary treatment for cancer, some people bring importance to their work. But others, including some work lovers, need to have the importance of their work reflected back to them. If others view their work as important, and respond accordingly, they are better able to value what they do themselves—and consequently take greater joy in their work.

Pastoral counselor David Hogue, for example, says he didn't fully appreciate the importance of his work when he first started out. "If you asked me today to rate the importance of my work on a scale of one to ten, I'd say nine and a half or ten," he says, "but I'm sure I didn't think of it as that important originally. I remember talking with a colleague about my frustration with a client who was having difficulty terminating our counseling relationship, and he said to me, 'I'm not sure you understand how important this has been for her.' That was pivotal for me in realizing the impact and change that pastoral counseling can bring to people's lives—how important it can be in bringing people to emotional and spiritual maturity. I also remember watching a colleague talking about the gratitude he received from clients—and he was in tears. I was intrigued by that, by how much it meant to him. Since then I've had cases where it's felt like a privilege to be there when something really important happened. It feels like what I imagine a midwife feels. When it happens, it's incredibly powerful."

For some work lovers, the importance of their work is reinforced by the fact that they get paid—if indeed they do get paid. As corporate trainer Barbara Daly says, only semi-facetiously, "I know my work is important because they pay me well for what I do."

There is a wonderful affirmation in getting paid to do something you enjoy. And, for many people, it's easier to enjoy work for which you are getting paid. Somehow it seems more important than the work that you do for free, even work that you do for free because you love it. The fact that others value your work enough to give you money to do it can be a gratifying confirmation that your labors have worth. Not all work lovers need this confirmation, but those who do find that it enhances their love of their work.

They've Been Obedient to God's Call

When people who love their work talk about the importance of their work, they often speak of a sense of supernatural calling, of obedience to God's direction. Author Karen Mains puts it very simply: "My work is important in that I'm obedient to what God has put in my heart."

Dean Leuking, senior pastor of a large midwestern Lutheran congregation, is very conscious of the role that his sense of call plays in his attitude toward his work. "My love for my work rests on the belief that what I'm doing is not just my idea," he says. "It's the result of a larger providence and the call of God." For Dean, the call of God came in an almost classic way.

"In August of 1945, following my high-school graduation, I was doing summer work on my uncle's farm," recalls Dean. "I went to a Sunday evening mission festival service in a small country church near Rochelle, Illinois, and the preacher that evening preached on the pastoral ministry and the call to ministry.

"The next day I wrote a penny post card home that said, 'The alfalfa looks good. How's the dog? How is the Kansas City baseball team doing? I think I'd like to be a pastor.' And that was all.

"I went home a week later, and on Friday night I talked with my own pastor. He told me about a school I hadn't heard of before, and by dawn the next Saturday morning I was on my way to Winfield, Kansas and to preparation for pastoral ministry."

Pastoral counselor David Hogue says his strong sense of call gives his work a continuing sense of importance. Ironically, David originally experienced what he believed was a call to the mission field. "At the end of my sophomore year in college, I was involved in a mission trip to Haiti," he recalls. "I came back from that trip, as many people did, convinced that my call was to the mission field. I think that sense lasted about five months for me and then became a more general sense of call to ministry.

"That personal sense of call just doesn't go away," David continues, his voice soft. "I still have a sense of mission about my work that gets me through when I can't see results."

A sense of call isn't restricted to work lovers whose vocations are overtly religious. Take Barbara Daly, corporate trainer for a large Chicago bank. She says that a sense of call is an important variable in her love of her work. But she experiences the call of God in a less overtly supernatural way. "Do I feel called?" she asks herself. "Yes, I do. Because I feel there is something important to be done and I have the right kind of skills to do it." Then there's businessman Ken Smith: "I've never had any idea that I am where I am, doing what I do, just because it's a way to make a living—but because it's where he has put me. As much as a missionary on any mission field, as much as a pastor in any church, as much as any so-called full-time Christian worker, I am also called. And that gives my job tremendous worth."

They're Using Their Gifts to Glorify God

"Long ago," says pastor Melicent Huneycutt, "I came to the realization that what glorifies God most is being the person I was created to be."

What a simple yet elusive idea: God is glorified when we are being the people he created us to be. If we use our God-given gifts in our work, we are glorifying God—which makes our work very important, indeed.

For illustrator Jack Stockman, the knowledge that he is using the gifts God created in him is a strong affirmation that his work is important. "God gave me an ability to be an artist, and I have a responsibility to glorify him with it," Jack says. "I've been given a gift, and if I don't click into that gift, I'm not operating the way God wants me to operate."

Operating the way God wants him to operate makes his work important, says Jack, even when he feels the *content* of the work is not inherently important. "Some projects I work on seem to glorify God more overtly than others," he says. "For example, I did some work for a book by Karen Mains that talked about allegorical relationships with God. That book will probably impact people more spiritually than a lot of the advertising projects I do. But who knows? Maybe if I do good work for an art director, even an art director I don't think is very good, and if I try to make that work come to life, maybe God is using me as an ambassador. Maybe in the long run that's more important than the work I do that is 'Christian.' "

In the movie *Chariots of Fire*, Olympic athlete and aspiring missionary Eric Liddell tells his sister, "God made me for China . . . but he also made me fast. And when I run, I feel his pleasure." It's tempting to think, as Liddell's sister apparently did, that his missionary work in China was more important than the time he spent churning around a track. But he believed that God gifted him to be a runner as well as a missionary. That belief gave his running tremendous importance. And the knowledge of God's pleasure gave *him* great pleasure.

They See Their Work as Part of a Larger Spiritual Agenda

"In order to love your work," says David Orth, "I think it has to be part of something that is bigger than itself. I love the technical stuff of woodworking, but it eventually becomes tedious. So for me, beauty is the larger thing from which my work gets its value. Beauty is greater than woodworking, so when I see a table, I'm not just seeing nice joints. I see beauty. Or at least sometimes I do. I've seen furniture that has nice joints in it, but no beauty or focus or spirituality.

"Even beauty eventually becomes tedious," David continues, "if it's not part of something bigger than itself. I think of it as something small within a series of larger concentric circles. Beauty makes me see my woodworking as important, and wisdom makes me see beauty as valuable. Wisdom is useless without love; love is difficult without the larger circle of faith and gratitude. And gratitude, I think, is one of the main religious motives. So ultimately, the source of the importance I see in my work is the bliss that I feel in God."

Some work lovers, like David, see an almost mystical spiritual agenda in the doing of their work. Others see their work as part of a different kind of spiritual agenda—a ministry agenda.

"Ministry" is a recurring theme in the conversation of many work lovers—at least those who are people of faith—when they describe the importance of what they do. They say their work is important because it is a *vehicle* for ministry.

"I see myself as a co-minister with the pastor," says John Folkening about his work as a church music director. "The real cement that holds our Christian community together is our worship life. I can't make 800 calls a week, but I can contact 800 people on a weekend through worship. As the hymns and liturgy come to life in worship, it gives people in the congregation the strength to go out and live their lives. And that puts my work on a par with anything I can think of."

"My work would be a lot easier to do if it weren't a ministry," says professional musician and radio personality Sandy Rios. "But it is. And I take it very seriously. Every time I do a radio program I think, *This is a responsibility. I can't just chitchat.* I have fun, but I'm also very aware that what I'm doing is important. When I directed the choir at the nursing school, I poured my life into those girls. I loved them and nurtured them and did the best I could to disciple them. I wasn't just leading a choir. I don't think I've been all that successful in my career. I don't have a Grammy. There's a lot of places I haven't been invited. But I've seen a lot of people's lives changed. I've seen people moved and touched. And that makes me feel that what I do is important."

Tim Botts, graphic designer: "When I came into the Christian publishing field, there was so much shoddy, backward stuff being done that I was ashamed of it. I thought, 'If I'm ashamed of it, how many people are being turned off by the message because it's being presented so poorly?' Because Christianity is so important, I feel it's very important that what I design is as excellent as possible."

Robert Gross, chiropractor: "To me, chiropractic medicine is tremendously important because it has to do with the controlling factors in the body. It's working toward a society that sees less disease, that isn't addicted to drugs, whether pushed or prescribed. It finally comes down to getting people to understand that their bodies are special, that God didn't put human bodies together like this to have them polluted with drugs, to not be taken care of."

When your work is not just a job, but a ministry, as it is for these work lovers, it feels important.

They Have a Mission

I'm struck by a quality that characterizes some of the people I talked with who seemed to love their work with the greatest intensity: a palpable sense of mission. These people have fire in their guts. They have a clear vision of what it is that they want to accomplish. They are not driven but *pulled* forward by a conviction that what they are doing is right. That it needs to be done. That it is important.

Businessman Gary Ginter, whom I mentioned earlier in this chapter, is a man with a mission. When he talks about his mission, he speaks so quickly and urgently that it's hard to keep up:

"I want to see a rediscovery of the old Moravian vision of the laity doing the work of God in crosscultural situations," he says, "of the laity using *all* of their gifts—those we call secular today and those we call religious. The Moravians flatly denied that distinction. When they sent out communities to carry the gospel to a new area of the earth, they ordained and laid hands on bricklayers and carpenters and tailors right along with evangelists and pastor/teachers. Under Count Zinzendorf, the Moravians set up businesses as their vehicle for mission, which created a much more transferable concept of what it meant to be a convert than the faith mission idea of, 'You go and I'll send money.' It offered a whole life view lived out in front of people.

"I would say my life had been successful if, when I die, there is a footnote in the idea pool from which young people draw their models for going into crosscultural mission—if there is a modern application of the Moravian vision of business and mission being done together naturally. If there's one young couple that thinks about the possibility of not only being in business in response to God's calling, but doing that in a crosscultural setting among an unreached people with the explicit intent of being a vehicle by which the gospel can flow to those people, I will consider myself a success.

"I want to see some young people discovering that, by being what they are—called of God and gifted to be businesspeople—they can simultaneously affirm that they are as much called by the Great Commission as any professional career missionary. I would challenge young people who are gifted as entrepreneurs to be stewardly entrepreneurs—and to see that as a valid alternative to going to another country as a traditional missionary."

145

They Have a Vocation

One word I almost never heard a work lover mention was "career." Considering that the topic of our conversations was work, that's a curious thing. Especially given the fact that our culture seems to be obsessed with *career,* a word that connotes climbing the ladder for its own sake. But most people who love their work don't seem to think about their work in those terms. Rather, they seem to think of their work as an expression of who they are, as a natural part of the total part of their lives—as a vocation.

Listen to the reflections of Martin Marty on the subject of vocation:

"Colleges today are good at shaping people who are good at picking up work, which they put inside a job. 'I have to go to *work* today because I have a job.' *Job* fits inside *career,* which has a longer trajectory than a job, but is still only a job. Next, a longer dimension of career tends to be *profession.* And profession fits inside *vocation,* which is the entire shape of a life.

"José Ortega y Gasset said that a person's vocation is to live a full, integrated, organic life in community and not to be obsessed with the social schema of a career. But what one sees around colleges is that career seems to interest young people the most. Because of their projected career they will work hard and have a job, but it's the career that matters. They are obsessed with career.

"The problem is, careers often get shattered. We see fifty-five-year-old executives out on the street. But if they have a vocation, they can find a new way to apply it."

Marty says he observed firsthand what can happen when a person with a vocation loses his career. "A man I know was president of a steel company when it was bought out by another firm," he says. "He was phased out of management. He was fifty-two years old and he didn't have any role. So he came to various people, including me, and said, 'What's next?' He was undoubtedly well off enough that he didn't need a huge income, but he needed the meaning of work. I knew he had a vocation, so I helped put him in touch with some like-minded people and he's now on the board of an innovative not-for-profit organization which is helping people in underdeveloped countries.

"In his role as a board member, he took us on a trip to Central America to see the results of the work of the organization. I watched him in action with tortilla makers and bakers, and I could just see the president of that steel company the day he took me down to the melting plant where he'd started out. We'd run into a big hefty guy driving a lift truck and my friend had said, 'How are the grandchildren?' He remembered the names of all of them. And he was the same person with the people in the foreign country. Even though he's not getting paid to be president of a steel company, he has a vocation."

Like this former CEO, like Martin Marty, like Gary Ginter and Ron Nikkel, like the others mentioned here, people of faith who love their work have more than a job. More than a career. More than a profession. They have a vocation. And that's why they believe their work is so important.

If you want to love your work, find out why it is important. It may be important because it benefits society. Or it's a response to God's call. Or it expresses your gifts. Or meets a need.

Perhaps it generates an important response. Or it's part of a larger spiritual agenda. Or you're able to see it as a mission or ministry.

If your work is important, it is part of your vocation—the entire shape of your life which has been shaped by God. And work that is part of your vocation—work that God created you to do—is almost always work that you can love.

14

Is It Really Possible to Love Your Work? Perspectives from Two Life Journeys

---

IN THE PRECEDING CHAPTERS, I'VE TOLD YOU ABOUT WHAT I'VE COME to believe are the secrets of people who love their work. But if you're naturally skeptical, as I am, at this point you may be asking yourself questions like these: Are the work lovers whose stories appear in these pages merely the exceptions who prove the rule that we humans will always labor by the "sweat of our brows"? Are most of us destined to experience at least as much frustration as fulfillment in our work lives? Is the search for lovable work ultimately an elusive one?

Or did God create each of us to exercise a particular set of gifts—such that opening ourselves to being the person God created us to be will naturally lead us to doing the kind of work we can love?

Sincere people of faith differ in their answers to these questions—perhaps because of their own life journeys.

In previous chapters, I've given brief insights into the life stories of almost fifty different people who love their work. But perhaps more can be gained from taking a closer look at some of these stories.

The journeys of two people of faith—each work lovers in their own way—may be instructive for those of us who are still trying to decide if the quest for lovable work is one we want to make—or should make. So here they are: the stories of two people who made crucial choices, choices that changed their work lives forever.

Cautionary Words from a Sometime Work Lover

Publishing executive Harold Myra is reluctant to describe himself as a work lover. Not that he doubts his calling. He believes he is probably in exactly the right spot as president of Christianity Today, Inc., a thriving magazine publishing company. He's been able to launch several successful magazines, nurture the careers of some talented writers, and guide CTi to fiscal strength—all of which is satisfying. But despite his successes, says Harold, he often doesn't enjoy his work on a daily basis. And even though there was a time when he did love his work without reservation, he doesn't believe enjoyment should be one's primary goal in work.

I've always been fascinated by writing. When I was in college, one of my professors used to say he didn't need to look for my name on the paper—he could just look for the thickness of the document. So when I entered a magazine's short story contest when I was in college and was fortunate enough to win, that was a great spur and goad and positive affirmation. After college, I joined *Youth for Christ* magazine as an editor and loved it. As a young bachelor, I did nothing but work, and I loved every minute of it. Learning the magazine trade. Learning how to use words to impact people. Learning journalism techniques and so on. But then I came to a point, after I'd become editor of the magazine, when I was asked to take over publishing responsibilities instead of just being an editor.

That was a fork in the road. I'm not a sales type at all. I don't enjoy imposing my will on other people. But I finally said yes to the larger role for two reasons. One, somebody had to do it and I felt that I probably could do it as well as others who might be considered. Second, when you're a creative individual, it's important to make sure that your environment is going to lend itself to creativity. And I was interested in holding my own destiny in that regard, rather than having someone else hold my destiny. Plus, there was a certain excitement to the idea of publishing magazines and learning something new.

But every decision has its up sides and down sides. If I had said, "No, I'm going to be an editor," I would have done things very differently in my life, and it probably would have been a good road. I would have ended up writing more books—probably at least ten science fiction books by now. And that's something I sometimes want to be doing. I find it more satisfying to do something personally creative on a daily basis. But if I had taken the other road I would have lost enormous other things that I've gained. I feel what I'm doing now is effective. I'm providing an environment for creative people, and it just may be that if I hadn't been in these particular places at these particular times, certain magazines wouldn't exist right now. It's a team effort, but we've been able to bring together a number of magazines and that has paid off for me—although the result gives me more satisfaction than doing it.

I like working with people, but I don't like many aspects of administration. One of my colleagues said to me at the coffee pot the other day, "Leadership is just taking care of messes." He was talking about church leadership, but it's true of any kind of leadership. You basically go from mess to mess, because people are people. So you face administrative difficulties. Some people just love that kind of thing. But I don't enjoy confrontation and some of the other components of administration.

Do people enjoy it when they're climbing a mountain and it's the third day and they're barely able to catch their breath and their hands are trembling? I don't know if the word *enjoy* fits there. They rise to the challenge. I guess that's the way I feel about my work. I feel life is warfare. You look around and almost everybody is bleeding today. But to be part of the warfare and to be doing something meaningful—I'm not sure that brings enjoyment, but perhaps a feeling of significance.

I see the world as a very difficult place in which to function undisturbed. The nature of life is such that it's extremely rare for people to be allowed to do what they really love. There are those rare people, maybe one out of a hundred—the writers who are good enough, the painters who are good enough—who are able to do what they want to do on their terms and in their structure. I think that's wonderful, but I don't think it can be projected as something that most people will experience. I think it's more like grace. You don't get that wonderful feeling of grace all the time— you get mountain tops. I think for most people it's the same way with work—you get those occasional mountain top times of really enjoying your work.

For me, the greatest joy is watching people develop. I've been privileged to work with some tremendously talented people, and being able to provide a structure in which they can grow and develop has been a point of great joy. I think that's what keeps me in my present work—I feel a responsibility and a duty. I feel a call.

I think people are happy and fulfilled when they have a purpose larger than themselves. There's a part of me that would just like to write. Because when I'm writing, I'm fully enjoying my work. But I feel called to this place. I feel a duty to this place. And to me, the duty has to come above enjoyment of work.

I think, too, that there is an expectation that has been set up in our generation that can be very destructive—that it is one's right to enjoy one's work, that one is enfranchised to enjoy one's work. I think the old idea—that you work to provide for your family and enjoyment comes as a side product—was a lot healthier. I think if you go to work expecting, my goodness, I've got to be fulfilled, you're a lot more likely to jump from job to job in an elusive search for something that will fulfill you.

I think a sense of well-being comes, first and foremost, from knowing we're on the track we're called to be in. And then, sometimes, a lot of enjoyment comes with it.

I made a choice between editing and publishing years ago. I've often said, you get opportunities and you wish you could be an amoeba, that you could split and follow two paths. But you have to choose one and shun the other. The truth is, despite the down sides, I've probably followed my star. I've probably taken the preferred path, even though there are a lot of parts of my job that I don't enjoy.

You have to make choices. You have to ask yourself some questions: What am I like? What kind of person am I? Can I take risks? Is taking risks good for me? Or am I really going to be a lot happier staying where I am and refining my skills and being able to apply them in other ways if this job dries up? You should certainly try to find those things at which you really excel. If it isn't something you can make a living doing, find something that's at least enjoyable to a degree. And then have an intensity about it.

For me, getting stretched has largely been a good thing. It's opened up vistas. It's been good for me, even though I would often prefer to go to the mountain top with my yellow pad. I think I've found my niche, even though I don't enjoy my work all the time. Probably over half the time I don't enjoy it. But I feel blessed that

I'm able to enjoy my work as much as I do.

One Man's Journey to Lovable Work

Dick Sawdey's story is in some ways the opposite of Harold Myra's. Myra started out loving his work and, in the process of pursuing what he believes is his calling, traded much of his enjoyment of work for a sense of significance and the satisfaction that comes with doing one's duty. Sawdey, on the other hand, didn't become a work lover until mid-life—when he began an intentional pursuit of what he believed was his calling.

By the time he reached his mid-forties, Dick already had what a lot of people want: a prestigious job in a respected company, a comfortable income, job security. But as each year passed, he was becoming increasingly dissatisfied. He wasn't enjoying his work as much as he thought he should. He knew he needed a change, but what kind of change? Was he in the right profession? Was he in the right kind of environment? Was it even realistic to hope that he could love his work? Or was he chasing an impossible dream? Listen as he tells his own story.

I decided to become an attorney when I was in high school and stayed with the decision in college, taking a pre-law program as an undergraduate. My initial move in that direction was partly a process of elimination. There were a number of fields I knew I wasn't suited for—engineering, science or things like that. I didn't know much about lawyers (we didn't have any in our family), but I knew that some of the skills they used were things I was good at—reading, comprehending, analyzing—intellectual pursuit as I understood it at the time. And I got some encouragement from my mother. She didn't tell me I ought to be a lawyer, but she confirmed some of my skills.

So I went to law school and enjoyed the education very much. I didn't have any idea really what lawyers did. But after graduating, I started with a law firm in Chicago and began to learn. It was somewhat intimidating at first, but exciting, and I found that the scope of work within the practice of law was much greater than I had comprehended. After several years in a law firm, I moved to a corporate setting and remained there close to fifteen years, serving in a corporate secretarial function—which is a mix of law and some internal management responsibilities.

By my late thirties and early forties I began to reflect on my life up to that point. I said to myself, "My life is about half over. Where am I? What am I doing?" I came to the realization that I was living out the decisions I'd made when I was roughly twenty years old. I'd achieved a fair degree of success. I had a home. I had security. My children were getting into the college years, so I'd accomplished the task of raising them. So what's next?

I knew I was dissatisfied with what I was doing, and I knew I would become increasingly dissatisfied as time went on. I could see why, but I wasn't really very sure what to do about it. I went through a period of several years where I knew some change was in order, but I really didn't know what it was. I had some ideas about what it was, but they weren't the right ideas. I sort of sensed that, and consequently I wasn't really actively pursuing them, but I knew I was looking.

I began something of a quest. I started reading things and interacting with people. I worked with the Myers-Briggs Typology Indicator, which was a very helpful tool for me, because it gave me insights about my creativity, problem-solving and conceptualizing—and tips on directions I ought to consider in terms of finding the things that gave me satisfaction and trying to maximize those in a job setting. My quest wasn't a Lone Ranger quest. I did a lot of interacting with people, one-on-one and in small group settings. It wasn't always intentional, but my antennae were out all the time and I was picking up thoughts and ideas.

At one point I began to think in terms of a job search and I worked, somewhat unenthusiastically, on a résumé. Then I called an acquaintance in the executive search field, told him where I was at, and asked if we could meet after he'd had a chance to look at my résumé. And he agreed to do that. So we had a lunch meeting one day in early December 1987. And I was very frustrated by our encounter. I was looking for some concrete ideas, maybe even a job position I could consider. But he really wasn't very interested in critiquing my résumé. He kept pushing me about whether I'd really considered who I was and what I wanted to do.

I thought I'd put these questions behind me. I felt I'd done my work. But he wouldn't let go of it. He asked me about my law practice days, about the things I'd enjoyed before going into the corporate setting. And I told him I'd enjoyed working with clients where I had a relationship with them, where I was, in effect, their lawyer. On a day-to-day basis, if they had a problem, they called me. We had a continuity, a relationship over a period of time, and I found that satisfying.

So he finally asked me, "If you could do anything you want, regardless of how feasible you think it is or whether it's financially sensible or not, no holds barred, what would you want to do?"

Answering that question was the first time I articulated having my own law practice. I said, "I'd just like to have a base of clients and serve them on an ongoing basis and have my own law practice. I'd really love that, but it's out of the question. I just don't see myself doing it." But we started talking about that, and he started encouraging me by pointing out possibilities of how that might be done. But when we broke up our meeting, I was despondent because I felt I hadn't gotten anywhere. I had a lot of confusion, and I thought the idea of my own law practice, while attractive, was out of the question. All I could see were the negatives—giving up financial security, a salary. Besides, I hadn't practiced law, strictly speaking, in years. I had a pretty good network of people I knew in the city so I could see where clients might come from, but, honestly, I just thought it was absurd. So I went back to my office in a lot of turmoil.

Over the course of the next few weeks, I continued to process all this, and it began having an emotional effect on me. I found myself daydreaming. I'd visualize myself in my own law office. I started asking other people for input. I'd ask, "How do you determine God's call? How do you determine if you're being called to something?" And one of the tests that was suggested to me was this: "If an idea is giving you a lot of energy, that's a pretty good sign to pay attention. It's not foolproof and it's not the only test, but it can well be a sign that God is calling you in a particular direction." When I heard that, I thought, *That's what's happening here. God's a lot smarter than I am. Maybe I ought to pay attention.*

So I paid attention and explored the idea of setting up my own law practice. I started listing some of the people I knew in private practice, either sole practitioners or people who had made some significant transition in their life from one career to another, say from a corporate setting to a law practice setting or from a big firm to a small firm. I began to contact these people and meet with them, just to hear their stories. And it turned out that their stories had a pattern. The pattern was: They took a risk. They went in a direction that was new, sometimes because they were forced to—something changed or was lost or they were terminated from a job. They went through a period of struggle, perhaps several years, and emerged loving what they were doing. All were doing well, all loved what they were doing. It was a great encouragement to me. I could look at them and say, *I'm as smart as they are. If they can do it, I can do it.* It got down to the basics of, well, would you do it? Are you willing to do it? Do you have the courage to do it, or are you not willing to make the sacrifices? That kind of put it on the line. I said to myself, *I'm not really driven to pursue a high degree of financial security. I'd like to make a decent living, but I have a lot of my basic obligations covered. My children will be able to go to college regardless of my decision.* My wife was returning to work, and she was supportive of the process of what I was doing and of any decision I made. I asked myself, *What is the worst thing that could happen? I could make a lot less money than I've been making. It might not work. What if it doesn't work? Well, I'll get a job. I'm not going to die. It's not a terminal illness.* And so I finally crossed the last internal, emotional barrier and made a firm commitment to do it. This is what I want to do.

Dick eventually quit his corporate job and established a working relationship with a small Chicago law firm, with the explicit goal of building his own practice. He shares office space—and some projects—with the attorneys in the affiliated firm but remains technically independent. His income has dropped considerably, but he's confident that it will continue to improve as his practice moves out of the start-up phase. Unlike several years ago, Dick is clearly enjoying himself. He exudes energy and enthusiasm. He says, without hesitation, "I love my work."

Given the success of his quest to find greater satisfaction in his work, I asked Dick to reflect on his own experience and assess what it was that he did right that others could emulate.

I think there was a combination of things I did right and things that happened around me. You could say that God created some concepts in me or an environment around me. I had an attitude of faith that allowed me to pick up on some things. I had the faith that loving your work is a goal that's achievable for everybody. Not everybody gets there, but I believe it's possible for everybody.

Even though my initial decision to pursue law was based mainly on my perception of external expectations, I eventually did a lot of work to discover what I now regard as my strongest gifts. I found that I have a strong interest in problem-solving, in using intuition to find solutions to problems. I like to conceptualize a situation, to be able to take data or facts or problems and be able to boil them down to their basics. To summarize and come up with theories or concepts about an approach, to then move forward and find the solution and put it in place. What I'm not good at, and what I don't derive energy from, is maintaining a structure once a solution has been arrived at. Ongoing administration is essentially about redundant, repetitive tasks. I'm not putting it down, because it's important. It's just not me. It tires me out. Other people ought to come in after I do what I do, and keep a structure going.

I also took risks. It was definitely a risk to quit my job. And I don't like risk. I'm a fairly risk-averse person. Which is why I didn't do this sooner. In my twenties and thirties, I was too fearful of financial insecurity or not confident enough in my own ability to do it. Having decided to do it, I can see the risk, but it's under control. I enjoy the degree of surprise that's part of each day. I enjoy not knowing where new situations are going to come up, where new clients are going to come from, what new problems existing clients will have. It's really a lot of fun. And I found that, once I made the decision to do this, people around me seemed to have a much stronger sense of the risk involved than I did. A lot of people told me, "That's a courageous decision." But by the time I made it public, it didn't feel courageous at all. It felt like the only possible thing I would want to do. I didn't have the feeling that it was a really gutsy move. But if I were in their shoes I can see how it might be perceived that way. And I think my decision created a little bit of envy in some people or at least raised issues for them, because I think a lot of people have gone through this process, but have shrunk back from what looks like a risky decision.

I was intentional about making my work an outgrowth of my faith life. I had a hard time finding a direct connection between my faith and the work I was doing before. I don't think I was avoiding God's plan for my life, but I also don't think my previous work had any particular connection to a call from God. But I definitely feel that what I'm doing now is a response to a call. I continue to feel a call and to respond to it. I believe I had a call because of how much energy I had for it and because I can see the fit between who I am as a person, the person God created, and the work I'm doing now. I really developed this idea while I was going through my quest. I thought a lot about work and faith, about work in the sense of vocation. I regard a person's vocation as far broader than what they happen to get paid for during the work day, but I wanted my work to be a fairly basic expression of who I was as a person. There's a sense in which I wanted my work to be a prayer. I wanted to be communicating and expressing and being the person God created as much as possible. In that sense, I feel my work is an expression of faith. Even though there are days when I work hard or long hours, it's not accompanied by stress, stress meaning being pulled in directions I know aren't me. That's very satisfying—to be doing that kind of work and to find yourself doing tasks that you get lost in and aren't aware that an hour went by while you're doing them. To be doing things in part that I'd do or would enjoy doing whether I got paid or not. So there are a lot of affirmations in my work that I definitely relate back to the life of faith.

I made some sacrifices. There's a sacrifice dimension to my story right now, for example, because I'm not getting a regular paycheck, and my income is down for the time being—and may never be what it was. I'm ready to face that. I'd like it to be more than it is right now, that's for sure. There's a degree of sacrifice in that, but I look at it more as deferring gratification—if the gratification is not only doing what you love, but also making an adequate living. I'm doing what I love, but I'm not making an adequate living. But I'm able to defer that because I have to go through a start-up phase. I'm not sacrificing in the sense of taking anything basic away from myself. But there's definitely a cost in doing this, a cost that I voluntarily accepted.

I made a conscious effort to arrange my work life so that I could have as much of a sense of community as I think I need. There's a part of what I'm doing that is an individual expression of who I am, and I don't want to water it down by working closely with someone else. I want my work to be something of an individualistic thing. But community *is* important to me and to be in this setting is important to me, where I have a community I can go to, people I can go to for help, assistance, knowledge and information. The people around me are supportive of me. They understand what I'm doing and the difficulty of it. And I have other communities. I have a small group I meet with monthly—people outside the firm—sort of a work-as-spirituality sharing group. They're people I have high respect for and we mean a lot to each other. We've been meeting for three years now, and in that time we've been able to support each other through all sorts of personal crises. In the first year, we shared our spiritual autobiographies with the group. And then in the second year, we shared our financial autobiography. We lost one person for awhile because of that. Money is a real taboo. Now we don't have a big topic or agenda, we just talk about where we're at in our life situations. It's a tremendous support for me. I like what I'm doing as an individual. But I like having a community to give me feedback, a community that allows me to share.

I also paid attention to the whole idea of place. I love having an office downtown. It would take a lot for me to relocate to the suburbs. In fact, I had a call last week from an attorney in the northern suburbs who wanted to have somebody else in the office with him. He talked to me about it a little, and I didn't give him an answer. But, as I think about it, I don't want to be there. I would be a five- or six-minute drive from my house, I could ride my bike to work, but I don't want to be in a residential suburb, and I don't think the kind of practice I want to develop could really be done from there. I just love being downtown. There's an excitement, a diversity, a chance to be with other people that I find very attractive. So place is a variable. It wasn't the variable that made me want to change jobs. But when I did make a change, I knew I wanted to be downtown.

As part of my inner work, I found out what kind of process was most satisfying to me. I realized I wanted a practice that was essentially oriented toward relationships with clients as opposed to a practice oriented toward transactions. A transaction orientation would mean, "What I love more than anything else is closing real estate deals or drafting wills," for instance. The satisfaction in that kind of practice would be in seeing how many of those you could do in a given period of time. You might deal with a client once and never see him again. Your reputation is, "This is the guy for real estate deals." What I prefer and what I'm building is a practice oriented to relationships with small businesses or individuals who have an ongoing need from time to time for legal services. I'm interested in building a relationship with them and working with them over a period of years, in getting to know them well and having the enjoyment of relating to them. That's a source of satisfaction. Another satisfaction is the problem-solving element. Using the knowledge or ability I have to help a person with a genuine need. In one case I was dealing with an executive who has a lot of stock options and other stock-oriented compensation. That's an area I have a lot of expertise in, and I was able to point out some potential problems so he could take some action ahead of time. He really appreciated that. I got a lot of satisfaction from having conceived an idea, presented it to a client, had him welcome it and deal with something in a preventive mode. So it's the process I enjoy—problem-solving in the context of relationships, foresight, communicating, helping people with their needs.

I would say that doing your inner work, as I did, is essential. You have to be able to discern how much of what you decide to do is based on what you perceive are the expectations of the outside world—other people, parents, friends, peers. Expectations that make you say, "If I'm going to be a lawyer, I have to be in a high-priced downtown firm, and I need these trappings externally to be successful." You have to get beyond that, to get down to the basics of who you are. There are a variety of ways to do that. The Myers-Briggs work was helpful to me, but so was reading and interacting with other people. I found an opportunity to grow. I think we are all in a sense growing, and if we're growing we have opportunities throughout life and mid-life to be moving more and more toward wholeness. Not everybody is conscious of that. Not everybody wants to be conscious of that. There's a dimension of it that's fear-producing. There's mystery. There are some people who have absolutely no interest in pursing any sort of self-exploration or for whom satisfaction seems to be entirely external. But for somebody who's serious about it, I'd say it's critical to do your inner work, to really take stock of who you are. Leave no stone unturned because you think it's impossible.

A Matter of Degrees

Harold Myra warns that seeking fulfillment from work is often an elusive search. Life being what it is, he says, work is bound to be frustrating and disappointing much of the time. It's misleading, perhaps dangerous, he believes, to hold out hope that it's possible for most people to love their work on a consistent basis.

Dick Sawdey, on the other hand, believes that most people *can* love their work if they're willing to take the journey to self-discovery—and act on what they find.

Who's right? Is loving your work the vocational equivalent of defying gravity—a rare abrogation of the laws of nature, laws which are the inevitable result of the fallenness of humankind? Or is it an achievable goal, one which most of us have a reasonable chance of attaining?

After talking with scores of people who say they love their work, at least an equal number who say they don't, and many more who say it depends on the day, I've come to this conclusion: Loving your work isn't an either/or proposition—it's more like a continuum. I've never met anyone who loves his or her work every minute of every day. Loving your work is a matter of degrees. What's more, getting fulfillment from work doesn't seem to be as important to some people as it is to others. For some folks, work is merely a means to an end, the source of a paycheck which makes it possible for them to get on with the business of living the rest of their life— the real part, the part they enjoy.

There's absolutely nothing wrong with that. But many of us long for more. We ask ourselves, *Am I headed for the right vocation? Or, Am I enjoying my work as much as I could? Is there some other job or profession out there that would bring me more satisfaction? Should I start actively looking for different work? Would a quest for more lovable work be an act of faith and courageous risk-taking—or a foolish and probably elusive exercise in windmill-tilting?*

I can't answer these questions for you. Each of us has to decide where we are—or, in the case of young people just starting out, are likely to be—on the enjoyment-of-work continuum and how important it is to us to increase the degree to which we love our work.

Harold Myra used to love his work, but decided there was something more important than enjoying what he did on a daily basis. Dick Sawdey was enjoying his work less and less, and decided life was too short *not* to enjoy what he did on a daily basis. Both made choices that were undoubtedly right for them.

At some point in life, most of us are faced with the choice of whether or not to pursue work we can love. For some of us, there may be good reasons—Harold Myra enumerates several of them— to choose against the pursuit.

But for those of us who decide to attempt the quest toward lovable work, it's important to know the secrets of those who have successfully completed the journey. These secrets, the secrets of those who can say without hesitation that they love their work, are simply stated, but not so simply achieved:

Hearing the Voice of God

Have you listened for the voice of God in seeking vocational direction? Have you allowed him to speak to you through others, through your inner voice and through circumstances?

Heeding Models, Affirmers and Mentors

Have you looked for models—people who can serve as examples to follow in shaping and pursuing your dreams? Have you listened to affirmers—people who help confirm God's call by pointing out your gifts and demonstrated interests? Have you sought out mentors—people who can show you how to pursue your dreams and, often, who give you an opportunity to do so?

Discovering Your Gifted Passions

Have you identified your gifted passions—your passionate interests which are supported by your gifts? If so, are you exercising them in your current work? If you have some gifted passions, but aren't using them in your work, or if you're a young person just starting out, have you considered how you might incorporate your gifted passions in a vocation? If you don't know what your gifted passions are, have you:

☐ Looked for clues in your childhood?

☐ Considered the areas in which you get affirmation?

☐ Tried the trial-and-error method (pursued your interests and waited to see if the results point to the existence of a gift)?

☐ Pursued vocational testing?

☐ Looked at the flip side of your perceived weaknesses?

☐ Let your gifts and passions find you?

☐ Paid attention to the activities that engage your most focused attention?

Identifying the Right Process
Have you learned what constitutes satisfying feedback for you? Do you know if you get more satisfaction from processes or results? Does your current work—or planned vocation—provide the kind of feedback you need? If not, can you find a way to get more satisfying feedback in your work?

Taking Risks
Are you willing to step out in faith in response to God's call? Are you willing to risk to pursue your vocational dreams? Are you willing to risk in the dailiness of living out your vocation?

Developing Competence
Have you taken the time and effort required to develop your natural gifts through practice, education and experimentation? Do you insist on increasing your level of competence even after you've achieved a measure of success?

Working in Community
Have you identified the degree to which you desire a sense of community in your work? Does your current work—or planned career—provide as much community as you feel you need or want? If you basically enjoy your work, but wish for more community, have you considered ways to combat isolation, such as:
☐ Joining a support group made up of other people in your profession?
☐ Scheduling regular breakfast or lunch meetings with friends or colleagues?
☐ Sharing an office with others in similar situations?

☐ Joining professional associations?

Making Sacrifices
Are you willing to sacrifice time, money, options, comfort, security, and/or prestige—at least for a time—in order to pursue work you can love?

Earning Enough Money
Does your work, or planned career, provide enough money to meet your needs? Do you currently feel well paid or have a realistic expectation of being, or feeling, well paid in the future? Have you identified how much money you would need to make to feel well paid? Are your expectations realistic?

Expressing Your Faith through Your Work
Do you view your work or planned vocation as an expression of your relationship to God? How does faith relate to the:
☐ motivation for your work?
☐ content of your work?
☐ manner of your work?
☐ results of your work?
☐ way you use your gifts?
☐ way you view your work in the context of your entire life?

Finding the Right Place
How important is "place" in your satisfaction with work? Which of the following is most important to you:
☐ Finding the right organization?
☐ Finding the right community?
☐ Finding the right physical environment?
☐ Finding the right niche within your profession?
   Are you happy with your current place? If you're just starting out,

have you thought about what place would be best for you?

Achieving Balance

Is your life balanced between work and other aspects of life (if you're just starting out, does your planned vocation allow for such balance)? If not, have you been able to find variety within your work, or do you have good reason to believe that you'll be able to achieve balance within a reasonable period of time?

Believing Your Work Is Important

Do you believe your work, or the work you plan to do, is important? Does it fit one or more criteria which many work lovers have identified as characteristics of important work:

- ☐ It benefits society.
- ☐ It's a response to God's call.
- ☐ It expresses your gifts.
- ☐ It meets a need.
- ☐ It generates an important response.
- ☐ It's part of a larger spiritual agenda.
- ☐ It's part of your personal mission or ministry.
- ☐ It demonstrates God's purposes for the world in your time and place.
- ☐ It fits within your vocation—the entire shape of your life which has been shaped by God.

If you are unable to reconcile yourself to the idea that work is, by its nature, unpleasant . . .

If you are on a quest for meaningful, satisfying work . . .

If you are looking for, not just a job, not just a career, but a vocation . . .

. . . then consider these principles and the questions they evoke. They are, I believe, the secrets of people who love their work. May these secrets help you to love yours.